FORTY HADITH
QUDSI

Translated by
Ezzedin Ibrahim & Denys Johnson-Davies

FORTY
HADITH QUDSI

SELECTED AND TRANSLATED

BY

EZZEDDIN IBRAHIM
B.A. (Cairo); (Ph. D. (Lond.)

DENYS JOHNSON-DAVIES
(ABDUL WADOUD)
M. A. (Cantab.)

IN THE NAME OF ALLAH
THE MERCIFUL THE COMPASSIONATE

Dar Al Taqwa Ltd. **January 2010**
ISBN 978-1-870582-72-8

All rights reserved. No part of this publication may be reproduced, stored in a retrieval system, or transmitted, in any form or by any means, electronic, mechanical, photocopying, recording or otherwise, without the prior permission of the publishers.

Selected and translated by
Ezzeddin IBRAHIM
Denys Johnson-DAVIES

Produced with special permission of the translator.

DAR AL TAQWA LTD.

Published by:
Dar Al Taqwa Ltd.
7A Melcombe Street
Baker Street
London NWI 6AE

Website : www.daraltaqwaonline.com
E-Mail : info@daraltaqwaonline.com

Printed by:
IMAK Offset Printing Center
www.imakofset.com.tr
isa@imakofset.com.tr

Contents

	Page
Introduction in English	7
Introduction in Arabic	24
The Hadith: Arabic text with English translation facing	40-147
Index to Hadith	149-152

**In the name of Allah
the Merciful the Compassionate**

INTRODUCTION

The present book, a selection of Hadith Qudsī[1] (i. e. the Sayings of the Prophet Muḥammad as revealed to him by the Almighty) with a translation into English, is a companion volume to our translation of the Forty Hadith of the Imām an-Nawawī. We thought it might be useful to preface the book with a short study about Hadith Qudsi (Sacred Hadith), their source books, the subjects treated, and the considerations taken into account when making our selection and preparing the translation.

Sacred Hadith are so named because, unlike the majority of Hadith which are Prophetic Hadith, their authority *(Sanad)* is traced back not to the Prophet but to the Almighty. The epithets *rabbānī* and *ilāhī* are also applied to them, both words giving the meaning of 'divine'.

Among the many definitions given by early Muslim

---

1. Hadith, often rendered as "Traditions", are the recorded words, actions and sanctions of the Prophet Muḥammad. The Arabic plural of the word *ḥadīth* is *aḥadīth* We have treated it as an English collective noun and have therefore not supplied it with the diacritical marks required by the rules of transliteration. In like manner we have preferred, in the title of the book, to retain the word "qudsi", it being a religious term, rather than to use its English equivalent. The meaning of the word *qudsī* is "sacred" or "divine" and throughout the Introduction we have employed the term Sacred Hadith.

scholars to Sacred Hadith is that of as-Sayyid ash-Sharīf al-Jurjānī (died 816 A.H.) in his lexicon *At-Taʿrīfāt* where he says: "A Sacred Hadith is, as to the meaning, from Allah the Almighty; as to the wording, it is from the Messenger of Allah, may the blessings and peace of Allah be upon him. It is that which Allah the Almighty has communicated to His Prophet through revelation or in dream, and he, peace be upon him, has communicated it in his own words. Thus the Qurʾān is superior to it because, besides being revealed, it is His wording."

A more comprehensive definition is provided by a later scholar, al-Mullā ʿAlī ibn Muhammad al-Qārī, the Hanafī jurisprudent (died 1016 A.H.) in which he says of Sacred Hadith that "it is that which is related by the foremost of relaters and the most reliable of authorities, the best of blessings and salutations be upon him, from Allah, may He be glorified, sometimes through the medium of Gabriel, upon whom be blessings and peace, and sometimes by revelation, inspiration and dreams, Allah having entrusted to him the expressing of it in such words as he wished. It differs from the Holy Qurʾān in that the revelation of the latter was only through the medium of the Upright Soul[1] and is restricted to the wording specifically revealed from the Preserved Tablet, which was then passed on by *tawātur*[2], absolutely

---

1. i.e. Gabriel.

2. A technical word meaning "the passing on or transmitting by groups of men" i.e. rather than by individuals. The manner in which the Qurʾān was recorded was by *tawātur*, while the majority of the Prophet's Hadith were passed on through chains of *āhād* (individuals).

unchanged in every generation, age and time. Many and well known are the consequences that flow from this: that [unlike the Holy Qur'ān] Sacred Hadith are not acceptable for recitation in one's prayers; they are not forbidden to be touched or read by one who is in a state of ritual impurity, or by a menstruating woman or one confined to childbed; if repudiated, such repudiation does not result in the person so doing being guilty of unbelief; and they are not characterised by the attribute of inimitability."[1]

It can thus be seen that, when dealing with Sacred Hadith, Muslim scholars throughout the ages have concerned themselves with clarifying the following four issues:

1. The distinction to be made between Sacred Hadith and Prophetic Hadith

As previously stated, the chain of authorities in the latter ends with the Prophet, while in Sacred Hadith the final attribution is to the Almighty. Generally, therefore, Sacred Hadith are to be found recorded in the first person. This does not of course mean that Prophetic Hadith are not based on divine inspiration, for it is said in the Holy Qur'ān[2]: "He does not speak by whim„

---

1. Among other definitions given by Muslim scholars are those of al-Ḥusayn ibn Muḥammad aṭ-Ṭībī (died 743 A.H.), Muḥammad ibn Yūsuf al-Kirmānī, the commentator on al-Bukhārī (died 786 A.H.), Ibn Ḥajar al- Haytamī, the commentator on an-Nawawī's *al-Arbaᶜūn* (died 974 A.H.) and Muḥammad ibn ᶜAllān aṣ-Ṣiddīqī, the Shafiᶜī scholar and commentator on *Riyāḍ aṣ-Ṣāliḥīn* (died 1057 A.H.).
2. Chapter 53, verse 3.

2. The distinction to be made between Sacred Hadith and the Holy Qur'ān

As indicated by al-Mullā al-Qārī in the above quotation, the Holy Qur'ān has been handed on down the centuries in its revealed wording by *tawātur* whereas Sacred Hadith have been transmitted in versions recorded by chains of individuals *(āhād)*. Sacred Hadith, moreover, are subject, in regard to establishing their authenticity, to the same stringent rules as are Prophetic Hadith, being regarded as sound and good or as weak and of doubtful authenticity according to whether they comply with the demands of these rules.

Minor differences between Sacred Hadith and the Holy Qur'ān, additional to those given by al-Qārī, include the fact that the Holy Qur'ān is divided into chapters and verses; that he who recites it is rewarded tenfold for every letter recited[1]; that the Almighty has promised that it will be preserved from change and alteration;[2] also that, when quoted from, the exact words should be given and not merely the meaning.

3. Whether the divine nature of Sacred Hadith extends both to the wording and the meaning

Scholars are divided in their opinions, some holding

---

1. See the Prophetic Hadith which says: "He who recites a letter from the Book of Allah will have a blessing, each blessing being as ten." It was related by at-Tirmidhī, who said it was a good and sound Hadith.

2. See Qur'ān, Chapter 15, Verse 9 which reads: "Truly We have revealed the Scripture and truly We shall preserve it.".

that both the meaning and the wording are from Allah the Almighty, supporting their view by the fact that Sacred Hadith are clearly ascribed to the Almighty, being called sacred or divine, also that the words of a Sacred Hadith are generally given in the first person. Other scholars interpret the same facts as showing that while the meaning is from Allah the Almighty, the actual wording is from the Prophet, duly authorised by the Almighty to provide the wording. Thus Sacred Hadith differ from the Holy Qur'ān in not possessing the attribute of inimitability, are capable of having variations in wording, and when being quoted the meaning may at times be given without necessarily giving the exact words.

With both schools in agreement that the meaning is from the Almighty, the divergence of thought between them regarding the wording consists in effect in the first holding the belief that the actual wording has been revealed, while the second school holds that it has been inspired. The difference is thus relatively slight.

4. The forms in which Sacred Hadith are recorded

Two main forms have been singled out by scholars for relating Sacred Hadith: the first—and that preferred by early Muslim scholars—being that the Sacred Hadith should start with the words "The Prophet, may the blessings and peace of Allah be upon him, says from among the sayings he relates from his Lord, may He be glorified", while the second form opens with the words "Allah the Almighty has said, from among the sayings related from Him by the Messenger of Allah, may the blessings and peace of Allah be upon him." The meaning is one and the same.

However, a study of Sacred Hadith reveals that they can also assume the following forms:

1. The Hadith starts with the words "The Messenger of Allah, may the blessings and peace of Allah be upon him, said that Allah, may He be glorified, said". This is a commonly used form[1].

2. The words of the Almighty are given in a form other than that of speech, as for instance in the Hadith where the words "My mercy prevails over My wrath" take the form of writing[2] and clearly refer to the Almighty.

3. Where the Hadith is not sacred from beginning to end but in which the sacred portion is clearly ascribed to the Almighty and follows introductory words by the Prophet explaining the particular circumstances in which the Hadith is being related[3].

4. The sacred portion of the Hadith is given within the whole Hadith and is ascribed to the Almighty in an

---

1. See Hadith 2 in the present collection.
2. See Hadith 1 in the present collection. A similar instance is the Hadith given by Muslim which reads: "Allah the Almighty revealed to me: You should behave humbly so that no one is haughty towards another and no one oppresses another." See, too, Hadith 39 of this collection.
3. See Hadith 7 in the present collection.

indirect manner e.g. by being introduced by some such words as "it is said"[1], it being clear from the context that the words that follow are those of the Almighty or are given at His bidding. Also the fact that the Arabic word *"yughfar"* (it is forgiven), which occurs in the same Hadith, is given in the passive voice, is a sure indication that in both instances reference is being made to the Almighty.

Of all these six forms, therefore, the first two traditional forms, together with the form "He said, may the blessings and peace of Allah be upon him, that Allah, may He be glorified, said" are employed when the Hadith is wholly sacred from beginning to end. The remaining forms are used in all other cases. All these forms are described as sacred owing to the presence in them of at least a phrase that is ascribed to the Almighty.

Sources and collections of Sacred Hadith

Sacred Hadith were not treated any differently from Prophetic Hadith in respect of the manner in which they were collected, tested and committed to writing. We thus find that the recognised books of Hadith are the sole sources of both types of Hadith, Sacred and Prophetic, no distinction being made between them and both being included under the classifications chosen by the compiler, apart from the particular formulae used in introducing Sacred Hadith and which have been referred to. It would seem that collections of Sacred

---

1. See Hadith 20 in the present collection.

Hadith as such were compiled only at a much later date. Such collections are not numerous and, to the best of our knowledge, comprise the following:

1. *Kitāb mishkāt al-anwār fīmā ruwiya ᶜan Allāhi subḥānahu min al-akhbār* by Shaykh Muḥyī ʾd-dīn ibn al-ᶜArabī (died 638 A.H.). The book contains a hundred and one Sacred Hadith and was printed in 1346 A.H. (1927 A.D.) in Aleppo. It may well be that this is the book referred to by Ibn Ḥajar al-Haytamī in his *Al-Fatḥ al-mubīn fī sharḥ al-Arbaᶜīn* when he says: "The Sacred Hadith are more than a hundred and have been collected in a large volume"—though Ibn al-ᶜArabī's 101 Hadith can scarcely be said to constitute a large volume.

2. In his books *Jamᶜ al-Jawāmiᶜ*, otherwise known as *Al-Jāmiᶜ al-Kabīr* and *Al-Jāmiᶜ aṣ-Ṣaghīr*, Jalālu ʾd-dīn as-Suyūṭī (died 911 A.H.) groups Sacred Hadith separately from Prophetic Hadith; this is due to the fact that the contents of the two books are arranged in alphabetical order and that those Sacred Hadith that begin with the phrase *qāla ʾllāhu ᶜazza wa jalla* appear under the letter "Q" (qāf). Sixty-six Sacred Hadith are given in *Al-Jāmiᶜ aṣ-Ṣaghīr* and a hundred and thirty-three in *Jamᶜ al-Jawāmiᶜ*.

3. *Al-Aḥādīth al-Qudsiyyah al-Arbaᶜiniyyah* by Mullā ᶜAlī al-Qārī (died 1016 A.H.). As its title indicates the book contains forty Sacred Hadith selected by the author; it was printed in Istanbul in 1316 A.H. (1898 A.D.) and again in Aleppo in 1346 A.H. (1937 A.D.)

4. *Āl-Ithāfāt as-Saniyyah bil -Ahādīth al-Qudsiyyah* by ᶜAbd ar-Raʾūf al-Munāwī (died 1031 A.H.), which contains 272 Hadith arranged in alphabetical order. It has been printed in Cairo several times.

5. *Al-Ithāfāt as-Saniyyah fī ʾl-Ahādīth al-Qudsiyyah* by Muhammad ibn Mahmūd at-Tarabzūnī al-Madanī, the Hanafī jurisprudent who died in the year 1200 A.H. (1795 A.D.) and is a different book from that of al-Munāwī's *al-Ithāfāt as-Saniyyah*. Al-Madanī refers to the fact that he had read the collections of both as-Suyūtī and al-Munāwī and had quoted from them[1]. It appears that the compiler attempted in his collection to bring together all the Sacred Hadith known to him; while his collection includes no less than 863 Hadith, he states that "a thorough search would lay claim to more than this."[2] However, the number contained in the collection includes numerous repetitions owing to the different versions given.

The compiler took the liberty of including in his collection a number of weak Hadith and even some which would be regarded by meticulous scholars as spurious; he does, however, draw attention to such instances.[3]

---

1. Muhammad al-Madanī: *Al-Ithāfāt as-Saniyyah fīʾl-Ahādīth al-Qudsiyyah*, page 39, Hyderabad edition of 1358 A.H.
2. Ibid., page 187.
3. Ibid., see for example the following Hadith: Numbers 110, 200, 201, 213, 316 and 327.

The collection was printed twice in Hyderabad, in 1323 A.H. (1905 A.D.) and again in 1358 A.H. (1939 A.D.); it was also recently printed in Cairo in 1387 A.H. (1967 A.D.).

6. In 1389 A.H. (1969 A.D.) a large collection of Sacred Hadith appeared in two volumes under the title *Al-Ahādīth al-Qudsiyyah*. Compiled by the Committee of the Qurʾan and Hadith of the Higher Council for Islamic Affairs in Egypt, the publication contains all the Sacred Hadith to be found in the six canonical collections[1] and in Mālik's *al-Muwaṭṭaʾ*. It is the most complete and reliable collection to date[2], containing as it does four hundred Sacred Hadith with different variants where they occur.[3]

Subject matter of Sacred Hadith

The subject matter of Sacred Hadith[4] is, by its nature, restricted, both by reason of the limited number

---

1. The collections compiled by al-Bukhārī, Muslim, at-Tirmidhī, Abū Dāwūd, an-Nasāʾī and Ibn Mājah.
2. If in a future edition the collection were to include, together with due verification, additional Sacred Hadith to be found in the Musnad of Aḥmad ibn Ḥanbal and other sources, the work could be regarded as truly comprehensive.
3. In 1397 (1978 A.D.) Muṣṭafā ʿĀshūr began publishing in Cairo a collection under the title "*Al-Aḥādīth al-Qudsiyyah*". Up to the present four short volumes have appeared containing 60 Hadith. The collection is attributed to the Imam an-Nawawī, though in fact the Imam an-Nawawī compiled no work with such a title; the book merely consists, as mentioned by the compiler himself, of Sacred Hadith extracted from the Ṣaḥīḥ of Muslim with an-Nawawī's commentary, together with some additions.
4. See:
   Aḥmad ash-Sharabāṣī: *Adab al-Ahādīth al-Qudsiyyah*. Ash-Shaʿb Press, Cairo 1969.
   Shaʿbān Muḥammad Ismāʿīl: *Al-Aḥādīth al-Qudsiyyah wa manzilatuhā fīʾt-Tashrīʿ*.
   W.A. Graham, *Divine Word and Prophetic Word in Early Islam*, pp. 95-101, Mouton, 1977.

of such Hadith and because of the divine utterances by which they are uniquely characterised and which confine them to particular domains to which they appear best suited.

It is possible, from an examination of them, to group the subject matter of Sacred Hadith under the following main headings:

1. Affirmation of the doctrine of Unity and being on one's guard against forms of polytheism and scepticism; revealing the majesty of the Creator and of His uniqueness in possessing the qualities of perfection and sublimity; and the furthering of right intention and sincerity when turning to the Almighty.

2. The proper discharge of religious observances, both those ordained and those recommended—including prayer, fasting, *zakāt*[1], pilgrimage, *dhikr*[2] and supererogatory works — with due devotion, humility and lack of self-interest.

3. The attainment of proper standards of morality and virtue; kindness towards one's relatives; good behaviour towards people in general; affection for the pious; and enjoining that which is good and censuring that which is objectionable.

4. Self-dedication to the cause of Allah through

---

[1] An annual tax levied on a man's capital wealth.
[2] The repetition of formulae in praise of the Almighty.

acceptance of such destiny as He has ordained; making oneself ready to meet Him; and willingness to give one's life and all that is dear to one in obedience to Him.

5. Preparation for the Day of Reckoning, with its rewards and punishments, through continual repentance and asking for His mercy; combining fear and hope; beseeching His pardon through such good deeds as one may have performed and through such intercession as He permits; total confidence in His abounding mercy which prevails over His wrath and enfolds His servants.

It is possible to generalise about the subject matter of Sacred Hadith and to say that they clarify the meanings of the Divinity and servitude to Him in its various aspects, particularly in the fields of belief, worship and conduct. They scarcely go beyond this domain into such areas as legislation, civil and commercial practices and the like, all of which are treated elsewhere, notably in the Qurʾān and Prophetic Hadith.

The style of Sacred Hadith is in keeping with its subject matter and can be said to take the form usually of direct expression, either by way of divine injunctions from the Almighty to His servants, or through verbal exchanges between Him and them, with spiritual guidance as their aim, or through such other forms of expression as will strengthen the bond between the Almighty and His servants. Whatever the form they take, the style of Sacred Hadith is invariably sublime, spiritual and deeply moving.

This is no doubt one of the reasons that has caused authors of books of *at-Targhīb wa ʾt-Tarhīb* i.e. of encouragement and admonition in religious matters, and of devotional and mystical works, to quote copiously from Sacred Hadith. Some, however, in doing so, have fallen into the error of failing to check the soundness of such Hadith and cite examples that are either weak or spurious when they could have made their choice from the corpus of those whose soundness has been established.

The present collection

During the last decade Sacred Hadith have attracted considerable attention: anthologies have been made of the Sacred Hadith to be found in the general books of Hadith, as previously mentioned; old collections that had been out of print have been reprinted; studies have been written about Sacred Hadith, their competence as authorities in religious matters and their validity as proofs in legal argument, or about the guidance and instruction they contain; and translations of them into other languages have been made for the benefit of those who do not know Arabic. In all these fields, however, there is still scope for further effort, and we have thus been encouraged to produce the present collection of a number of sound Sacred Hadith, together with a translation into English of their meanings. In the preparation of it the following considerations have been taken into account:

a.) that the number should be confined to forty, thereby following the practice of other compilers of short selections of Hadith who took as a guide the words of the Prophet (may the blessings and peace of Allah be upon him): "Whosoever memorises and preserves for my People forty Hadith relating to their religion, Allah will resurrect him on the Day of Resurrection in the company of jurists and religious scholars". It was moreover felt that a reasonably limited number would provide an easier introduction to the subject for those studying it and would encourage them to extend their readings in it further, and that a judicious selection of forty Hadith would none the less adequately cover a number of religious fundamentals.

b.) that great care be taken in checking the Hadith chosen so that the collection might contain only those that were of sound authority. Thus, among those chosen are thirty-four Hadith that are to be found in either one or both of the *Saḥīḥs* of al-Bukhārī and Muslim, while the remaining six, duly authenticated, are to be found in the other well known collections; such authentication is, where applicable, referred to in a note to the Arabic text of the particular Hadith.

When a Hadith is to be found in more than one source, as is mostly the case, we have first given the source from which we have taken the version used and have then mentioned the other sources in which it appears.

c.) that the Hadith chosen should patently possess the characteristic of being sacred, either by the text being sacred from beginning to end, or by the presence within the Hadith of a phrase that is sacred.

d.) that the Hadith chosen should as far as possible illustrate the various subjects covered by Sacred Hadith so that the reader may gain a general idea of their nature and the guidance they provide.

The Hadith have been arranged according to subject matter, starting with those dealing with faith and followed by those relating to religious observances, virtuous qualities and actions, martyrdom and forbearance towards what Allah has decreed, repentance and the asking of His mercy, and, finally, those Hadith that are concerned with the Day of Reckoning. The volume both opens and closes with Hadith that tell of the mercy and favour of Allah.

We were further encouraged to produce the present collection, together with a translation, by the fact that, to the best of our knowledge, only two books of Sacred Hadith have been produced in English translation. These are:

1. Hadees-e-Qudsi, selected by Maulana Ahmad Saeed Dehlvi and translated, apparently from the Urdu, by Mohammad Salman. It was printed in India in 1972 and again in 1976. Containing only the English translations, the Hadith vary in the degree of their

authenticity, some of them being weak. The translation is in need of proof-correcting and revision.

2. The third section of Dr. William Graham's *Divine Word and Prophetic Word in Early Islam* . It contains ninety Hadith in translation, together with the original texts. While the Hadith vary in their degrees of authenticity, they are all clearly traced back to their original sources. The book was published in America in 1977.

In translating the Hadith in the present collection we have followed the same procedure adopted with an-Nawawī's *Forty Hadith,* namely that we co-operate together, each one of us complementing the work of the other and acting as a check on him. This system has, we hope, helped in our attempts at attaining accuracy and precision; in undertaking the translation we have consulted the most reliable commentaries. At the same time we have striven to provide a readable English rendering.

In our translation of the meanings of the Sacred Hadith we have adhered closely to the original. When forced to depart slightly from a strictly literal rendering, we have indicated this in a footnote; when we felt obliged to add words to the English translation for the sake of style or clarity, we have enclosed such additions in square brackets. The word "Allah" has been retained and has not been translated as "God"; certain religious terms such as *zakāt* and *dhikr* have also been retained and explanatory notes supplied.

The original Arabic text has been printed alongside the English translation for ease of reference. The footnotes have been kept to a minimum.

It is our hope that we have been able to provide the Arabic reader, as also readers of English, be they Muslim or non-Muslim, with a collection of authenticated Sacred Hadith which will serve them as an introduction to this branch of devotional literature and will encourage them to acquaint themselves further with it.

May the Almighty make it possible for us to complete the other similar translations in the field of Hadith that we wish to carry out.

Praise be to Allah, Lord of the worlds.

Abu Dhabi on 1st Muḥarram 1400 A.H.
20th November 1979 A.D.

                              Ezzeddin Ibrahim
                              Denys Johnson-Davies (Abdul Wadoud)

✻✻✻

بِسْمِ اللَّهِ الرَّحْمَنِ الرَّحِيمِ

المقدمة

الحمد لله ، والصلاة والسلام على سيدنا رسول الله ، وعلى آله وصحبه ومن والاه ، وبعد .

فهذه مجموعة مختارة من الأحاديث القدسية ، نقدمها مع ترجمةٍ لمعانيها إلى اللغة الإنجليزية ، بنفس الطريقة التي اتبعناها من قبل عند تقدمة (الأربعين النووية) للإمام النووي .

ولعله من المفيد ، أن نقدم بين يدي هذه المجموعة ، دراسة مختصرة عن معنى الحديث القدسي ، ومصادره وكتبه ، والموضوعات التي يدور حولها ، ثم نبين الاعتبارات التي روعيت في اختيار الأحاديث وإعداد الترجمة .

معنى الحديث القدسي :

الحديث القدسي ، هو ضرب خاص من الأحاديث ، التي تروى عن النبي ﷺ ، فيسندها إلى الله عز وجل . وبسبب هذا الإسناد اكتسبت هذه الأحاديث صفة القدسية ، وقد تسمى أيضاً لنفس السبب الأحاديث الإلهية ، والأحاديث الربانية .

وقد وردت في بيان معنى الحديث القدسي طائفة من التعريفات والأقوال القديمة والمتأخرة التي تستأهل الإشارة .

فمن أقدم هذه التعريفات ، ما أورده السيد الشريف الجرجاني المتوفى سنة ٨١٦ هـ في كتابه (التعريفات) ، إذ يقول(١) : « الحديث القدسي : هو من حيث المعنى من عند الله تعالى ، ومن حيث اللفظ من رسول الله ﷺ . فهو ما أخبر الله تعالى به نبيَّه بإلهام أو بالمنام ؛ فأخبر عليه السلام عن ذلك بعبارة نفسه . فالقرآن مفضَّل عليه ، لأن لفظه منزَّل أيضاً » .

ومن التعريفات المتأخرة قول الملا علي بن محمد القاري الفقيه الحنفي المتوفى سنة ١٠١٦ هـ في مقدمة مجموعته (الأحاديث القدسية الأربعينية)(٢) : الحديث القدسي هو ما « يرويه صدر الرواة وبدر الثقات ، عليه أفضل الصلوات وأكمل التحيات ، عن الله تبارك وتعالى ، تارة بواسطة جبريل عليه الصلاة والسلام ، وتارة بالوحي والإلهام والمنام ؛ مفوَّضاً إليه التعبير بأي عبارة شاء من أنواع الكلام . وهي تغاير القرآن الحميد والفرقان المجيد : بأن نزوله لا يكون إلا بواسطة الروح الأمين ، ويكون مقيداً باللفظ المنزل من اللوح المحفوظ على وجه التعيين ، ثم يكون نقله متواتراً قطعياً في كل طبقة وعصر وحين . ويتفرع عليه فروع كثيرة عند العلماء بها شهيرة : منها عدم صحة الصلاة بقراءة الأحاديث القدسية ، ومنها عدم حرمة مسها وقراءتها للجنب والحائض والنفساء ، ومنها عدم كفر جاحدها ، ومنها عدم تعلق الإعجاز بها » .

───────────────
(١) الشريف الجرجاني/ علي بن محمد بن علي : (التعريفات) ص ٤٥ . الدار التونسية للنشر . تونس ١٩٧١م
(٢) ملا علي القاري : (الأحاديث القدسية الأربعينية) ص ٢ . المطبعة العلمية . حلب ١٩٢٧ م .

ومع هذين التعريفين تعريفات وأقوال أخرى قديمة ومتأخرة ، لا تكاد تخرج في مضمونها عما ذكر . منها تعريفات الحسين بن محمد الطِّيبي المتوفى سنة ٧٤٣ هـ ، ومحمد بن يوسف الكِرْماني شارح البخاري المتوفى سنة ٧٨٦ هـ ، وابن حَجَر الهَيْتمي شارح الأربعين النووية المتوفى سنة ٩٧٤ هـ ، ومحمد بن عَلّان الصديقي الشافعي شارح رياض الصالحين المتوفى سنة ١٠٥٧ هـ ، وغيرهم[1] .

وقد حرص العلماء من قديم على تجلية معنى الحديث القدسي ، بإيضاح أربعة أمور :

١ ـ التمييز بين الحديث القدسي والحديث النبوي : فالنبوي ينتهي سنده إلى الرسول ﷺ ، بينما يرتفع سند القدسي إلى الله عز وجل ، فالقول فيه له جل جلاله . وكثيراً ما يكون بضمير المتكلم ، كما في حديث تحريم الظلم : « يا عبادي ؛ إنِّي حَرَّمْتُ الظُّلْمَ على نَفْسي ، وجَعَلْتُهُ بَيْنَكُم مُحَرَّماً ، فَلا تَظالَمُوا .. » . وهذا لا ينفي أن الحديث النبوي يستند في مجموعه إلى وحي من الله ، لعموم قوله تعالى : ﴿وَمَا يَنطِقُ عَنِ الهَوَى﴾[2] .

٢ ـ التمييز بين الحديث القدسي والقرآن الكريم : وقد بيّن الملا علي القاري في النص الذي مر سابقاً أن القرآن الكريم منقول بلفظه

―――――――――
(١) انظر : المجلس الأعلى للشؤون الإسلامية : (الأحاديث القدسية) ج١ ص ٥ ـ ٧ . القاهرة ١٩٦٩ م .
ـ محمد بن علان الصديقي : (كتاب دليل الفالحين لطرق رياض الصالحين) ج١ ص ٧٤ ، ٢٠١ . دار الكتاب العربي . بيروت .
ـ د . شعبان محمد إسماعيل : (الأحاديث القدسية ومنزلتها في التشريع) ص ٢٨ . القاهرة ١٣٩٨هـ .
(٢) سورة النجم: آية ٣ وانظر فيها تفسير ابن كثير.

المنزل بالتواتر القطعي على مر العصور . أما الحديث القدسي فمنقول برواية الآحاد . ويخضع في إثباته لكل قواعد التمحيص التي تخضع لها سائر أحاديث الآحاد ، فيُصَحَّح أو يُحَسَّن أو يُضَعَّف وفقاً لتلك القواعد .

ومن الفروق الفرعية التي ذكرها العلماء ، إضافةً لما أورده القاري ، أن القرآن الكريم مُقسَّم إلى سور وآيات ، وأن قارئه يثاب على كل حرف بعشر حسنات[1] ، وأن الله تعالى قد تأذَّن بحفظه من التغيير والتبديل[2] ، وأنه لا يُروى بالمعنى ، ولا يثبت شيء من ذلك للحديث القدسي .

٣ ـ بيان الصفة التي ورد بها الحديث القدسي من جهة معناه ولفظه . وللعلماء في هذا رأيان : فمنهم من يرى أن المعنى واللفظ جميعاً من الله ، ويحتجون لذلك بأن الأحاديث القدسية معـزوّة صراحة إلى الله عز وجل ، وبتسميتها قدسية وإلهية وربانية ، وبورود الخطاب فيها بصيغة المتكلم . ومنهم من يرى أن المعنى وحده من الله لنفس هذه الأسباب ، وأما التعبير فهو من الرسول ﷺ بتفويض من الله . وبذلك جاءت عبارة الأحاديث غير معجزة، وقابلة لاختلاف الرواية ، وجائزة الرواية بالمعنى .

على أن هذا الاختلاف غير خطير ، فما دام الاتفاق قائماً على أن

---

(١) إشارة إلى قوله ﷺ :«مَنْ قَرَأَ حَرْفاً من كِتَابِ اللهِ، فَلَهُ حَسَنَةٌ، وَالْحَسَنَةُ بِعَشْرِ أَمْثَالِهَا. لا أَقُولُ آلم حَرْفٌ، وَلَكِنْ أَلِفٌ حَرْفٌ، وَلامٌ حَرْفٌ، وَمِيمٌ حَرْفٌ» الترمذي، وقال حديث حسن صحيح .

(٢) إشارة إلى قوله تعالى:﴿إِنَّا نَحْنُ نَزَّلْنَا الذِّكْرَ، وَإِنَّا لَهُ لَحَافِظُونَ﴾ الحجر: ٩.

المعنى من الله ، وعلى ارتفاع الاعجاز والحفظ عن التعبير اللفظي ، فلم يبق بعد هذا إلا أن يكون التعبير قد أُجري على لسان الرسول الأمين ﷺ أو جرى ، إما بإلهام وإما بتوفيق .

٤ ـ الصور التي تروى بها الأحاديث القدسية : استظهر العلماء لرواية هذه الأحاديث صورتين : إحداهما ، وهي المفضلة لدى السلف ، أن يُقال في صدر الحديث القدسي : « يقول النبي ﷺ ، فيما يرويه عن ربه عز وجل » ، والثانية هي أن يُقال : « قال الله تعالى ، فيما رواه عنه رسول الله ﷺ » والمعنى واحد .

على أن المتتبع للأحاديث القدسية في كتب الحديث ، يجد أن لها ، بالإضافة إلى هاتين الصورتين ، الصور الأخرى الآتية :

١ ـ أن يُصدَّر الحديث بعبارة « قال رسول الله ﷺ ، قال الله عز وجل » ـ ثم يُورد الحديث ، وهو كثير(١) .

٢ ـ أن يرد كلام الله تعالى في الحديث موصوفاً بعبارة غير القول ، كما في حديث مسلم « لمَّا قَضَى اللَّهُ الخَلْقَ ، كَتَبَ في كِتابهِ على نَفْسِهِ ، فَهُوَ مَوْضُوعٌ عِنْدَهُ : إنَّ رَحْمتي تَغْلِبُ غَضَبي »(٢) . وورود النص بصيغة المتكلم ، قطعي الدلالة في النسبة إلى الله تعالى .

٣ ـ ألا يكون الحديث قدسياً من أوله إلى آخره ، بل يرد فيه الجزء القدسي صريحاً في النسبة إلى الله ، ولكنْ بعد كلام للنبي ﷺ يُبين

―――――――――
(١) انظر مثلاً الحديث الثاني من هذه المجموعة .
(٢) الحديث الأول من هذه المجموعة . ومن ذلك أيضاً حديث مسلم « إن اللَّهَ تَعَالى أَوْحى إِلَيَّ أَنْ تواضَعُوا حتى لا يَفْخَرَ أحدٌ على أحَدٍ ، ولا يَبْغيَ أحدٌ على أحَدٍ » مسلم : ج٥ ص ٧١٨ . فكلام الله في الحديث الأول مقدم بلفظ (كَتَبَ) ، وفي الثاني بلفظ (أَوْحى) .وانظر الحديث التاسع والثلاثين من هذه المجموعة .

فيه مناسبة القول ، كحديث النسائي ، يقُول رسولُ اللّهِ صلَّى اللّهُ عليهِ وسلَّمَ : « يَعْجَبُ رَبُّكَ من رَاعي غَنَمٍ ، في رأسِ شَظِيَّةِ الجبلِ ، يُؤذِّنُ بالصَّلاةِ ويُصَلِّي . فيقولُ اللّهُ عَزَّ وَجَلَّ : انْظُروا إلى عَبْدي هَذا . . الحديث »[1]

٤ ـ أن يرد الجزء القدسي ، ضمن الحديث كما ذُكر ، ولكن عزوه إلى الله تعالى يُفهم من سياق الحديث ، لا بالنسبة الصريحة ، كما في حديث مسلم « قال ﷺ : تُفْتَحُ أَبْوَابُ الجَنَّةِ يَوْمَ الاِثْنَيْنِ وَيَوْمَ الخَمِيسِ ، فيُغْفَرُ لِكُلِّ عَبْدٍ لاَ يُشْرِكُ بِاللهِ شَيْئاً ، إلا رَجُلاً كانَتْ بَيْنَهُ وبَيْـنَ أخِيهِ شَحْنَاءُ ، فيُقَال : انْظِروا هَذيْنِ حتى يَصْطَلِحا . . الحديث »[2] فبالرغـم من عبـارة (يُقَـال) المبنية للمجهول ، فإن السياق يدل على أن القول لله تعالى ، أو بأمـره . ويؤكده ورود (يُغْفَر) بالبناء للمجهـول أيضاً قبـل ذلك ، والمغفرة من الله وحده[3] .

ويمكـن الجمـع بين هذه الصـور الأربـع ، والصورتيْن المشهـورتيْن المـذكورتيْن قبـلاً ، بأن هاتين الصـورتين ، هما الواردتان في الأحاديث التي يرد نصها قدسياً من أوله إلى آخره[4] ،

---

(١) الحديث السابع من هذه المجموعة .
(٢) الحديث العشرون من هذه المجموعة .
(٣) ومما يجري هذا المجرى عبارة (نادى مناد) أو (نُودي) بالبناء للمجهول ، ويدل السياق على أن النداء بأمر من الله تعالى أو من قبله . انظر ابن ماجه : حديث رقم ٤٢٠٣ ومسند أحمد : ج ٤ ص ٣٣٢ .
(٤) والأحاديث التي يرد نصها قدسياً من أولها إلى آخرها ، تغلب عليها صيغة المتكلم . ومع ذلك فقد ترد بصيغة الغائب ، كما في الحديث المتفق عليه رقم ١٦ من هذه المجموعة ، وهو قدسي بلا خلاف .

بالإضافة إلى صورة « قال ﷺ : قال الله عز وجل » أما الصور الأخرى ، فترد فيما عدا ذلك . وقد وصفت جميع هذه الصور والصيغ بوصف التقديس لاحتوائها جميعاً على عبارة معزوة إلى الله تعالى .

مصادر الأحاديث القدسية وكتبها :

عوملت الأحاديث القدسية من حيث الجمع ، والتمحيص ، والتدوين معاملة سائر الأحاديث النبوية ، وبذلك تعتبر كتب الحديث المعتمدة هي مصادرها الوحيدة ، ترد في ثناياها ، وفقاً لتبويبها ، ولا تتميز عنها إلا بورودها وفقاً لإحدى صيغها المعروفة .

ولا نعلم أن هذه الأحاديث قد تميزت بجمع مستقل في فترة التدوين الأولى للتراث النبوي ، وإنما ظهر ذلك في زمن متأخر . وما وصل إليه علمنا من مجموعات الأحاديث القدسية المستقلة التي طبعت هو ما يلي :

١ - « كتاب مشكاة الأنوار ، فيما روي عن الله سبحانه من الأخبار » للشيخ محيي الدين بن العربي المتوفى سنة ٦٣٨ هـ . وقد اشتمل الكتاب على مائة وواحد من الأحاديث القدسية ، وطبع سنة ١٣٤٦ هـ (١٩٢٧ م) في حلب . وقد يكون هذا الكتاب هو ما أشار إليه ابن حَجَر الهَيْتمي في (الفتح المبين في شرح الأربعين) بقوله « القدسية أكثر من مائة ، وقد جمعها بعضهم في جزء كبير »[1] ، وإن كانت المائة لا تشكل جزءاً كبيراً .

---

(١) ابن حجر الهيتمي : (الفتح المبين) . ص ٢٠١ . دار الكتب العلمية . بيروت ١٩٧٨ م

٢ - في (جمع الجوامع/ الجامع الكبير) و (الجامع الصغير) لجلال الدين السيوطي المتوفى سنة ٩١١ هـ ، تمييز للأحاديث القدسية اقتضته ضرورة ترتيب الكتابين وفقاً للحروف الهجائية . إذ ترد هذه الأحاديث تحت حرف القاف مبدوءة بعبارة (قال الله عز وجل) أو نحوها . وفي الجامع الصغير منها ستة وستّون حديثاً[١] ، وفي جمع الجوامع مائة وثلاثة وثلاثون حديثاً[٢] .

٣ - « الأحاديث القدسية الأربعينية » للمُلّا علي القاري المتوفى سنة ١٠١٦ هـ . وهي كما يدل عليه عنوانها أربعون حديثاً قدسياً ، اختارها المؤلف ، وطبعت في الآستانة سنة ١٣١٦ هـ(١٨٩٨ م)ثم في حلب سنة ١٣٤٦ هـ (١٩٢٧ م) .

٤ - « الاتحافات السنية بالأحاديث القدسية » لعبد الرؤوف المُناوي المتوفى سنة ١٠٣١ هـ وتحتوي على ٢٧٢ حديثاً مرتبة على حروف الهجاء . وطبعت في القاهرة عدة مرات .

٥ - « الاتحافات السنية في الأحاديث القدسية » لمحمد بن محمود الطَّرَبْزوني المدني الفقيه الحنفي المتوفى سنة ١٢٠٠هـ (١٧٩٥ م) ، وهي غير (الاتحافات السنية) للمناوي . وقد أشار المدني إلى أنه قد اطلع على ما جمعه السيوطي والمناوي ونقل

---

(١) عبد الرؤوف المناوي : (التيسير بشرح الجامع الصغير) . ج٢ ص ١٨٢ ، بولاق ١٢٨٦هـ .
(٢) جلال الدين السيوطي : (جمع الجوامع أو الجامع الكبير) . ج٢ ص ٥٩٤ نسخة مصورة . الهيئة المصرية العامة للكتاب القاهرة ١٩٧٨ م .

عنهما(١) . ويبدو أن المؤلف قد حاول أن يجمع في مجموعته هذه كل ما وصل إليه علمه من الأحاديث القدسية فجمع ٨٦٣ حديثاً ، وقال « والاستقراء يقتضي بأزيد من هذا »(٢) . على أن هذا العدد نفسه يتضمن مكررات كثيرة وفقاً لاختلاف الروايات .

وترخص المؤلف رحمه الله فأدخل في مجموعته عدداً من الأحاديث الضعيفة ، بل وربما أدخل ما اعتبره بعض المحققين موضوعاً ، إلا أنه قد نبّه على ذلك في مواضعه(٣) . وقد طبعت هذه المجموعة في حيدر آباد مرتين سنة ١٣٢٣ هـ (١٩٠٥ م) وسنة ١٣٥٨ هـ (١٩٣٩ م) وطبعت أخيراً في مصر سنة ١٣٨٧ هـ (١٩٦٧ م) .

٦ - وفي سنة ١٣٨٩ هـ (١٩٦٩ م) صدر مجموع كبير من جزئين بعنوان (الأحاديث القدسية) ، ألفته لجنة القرآن والحديث في المجلس الأعلى للشؤون الإسلامية بمصر . واستخرجت فيه الموجود من الأحاديث القدسية في الكتب الستة وموطأ مالك . ويعتبر هذا المجموع أوسع تأليف وأضبطه في هذا الباب حتى الآن(٤) ، ويشتمل على أربعمائة حديث بما في ذلك الروايات

---

(١) محمد المدني : (الاتحافات السنية في الأحاديث القدسية) . ص ٣٩ ط٢ ، حيدر آباد الدكن ١٣٥٨هـ .

(٢) محمد المدني : الاتحافات ص ١٨٧ .

(٣) محمد المدني : الاتحافات . انظر مثلاً أحاديث رقم ١١٠ ، ٢٠٠ ، ٢٠١ ، ٢١٣ ، ٣١٦ ، ٣٢٧ .

(٤) ولو استوعب هذا المجموع ، في طبعة قادمة ، ما يكون قد بقي في مسند أحمد وبقية مصادر السنة مع التحقيق ، إذن لأوفى على الغاية .

المختلفة لكل حديث إذا وجدت(١) .

موضوعات الأحاديث القدسية :

موضوعات الأحاديث القدسية بطبيعتها محدودة(٢) : فعدد هذه الأحاديث نفسها محدود ، والقول الإلهي الذي هو مضمون هذه الأحاديث له طابعه الفريد ومجالاته الخاصة التي تبدو أكثر مناسبة له .

ومن الممكن ، باستقراء الأحاديث القدسية الصحيحة التي وصلتنا ، أن نجمل مضامينها في الموضوعات الرئيسة الآتية :

تأكيد عقيدة التوحيد : وتخليصها من مظاهر الشرك والتشكك ، وبيان عظمة الخالق وتفرده بصفات الكمال والجلال ، والحث على صحة النية وصدق التوجه إلى الله .

٢ - حسن أداء العبادات : المفروضة والمندوبة ، من صلاة وصيام وزكاة وحج وذكر وتنفل - بكل إخلاص ، وإخبات ، واحتساب .

(١) وفي سنة ١٣٩٧هـ (١٩٧٨ م) بدأ مصطفى عاشور في نشر مجموعة بعنوان (الأحاديث القدسية) في القاهرة ، ظهر منها حتى الآن أربعة أجزاء صغيرة تشتمل على ٦٠ حديثاً ، وقد عزا المجموعة إلى الإمام النووي . والحقيقة هي أن الإمام النووي لم يؤلف كتاباً بهذا العنوان ، ولا تعدو المجموعة أن تكون ، كما ذكر المؤلف نفسه ، استخراجاً لما في صحيح مسلم بشرح النووي ، من الأحاديث القدسية ، مع بعض الإضافات .

(٢) انظر في هذا الموضوع :

- د . أحمد الشرباصي : (أدب الأحاديث القدسية) ، مطبعة الشعب . القاهرة ١٩٦٩ .
- د . شعبان محمد اسماعيل : (الأحاديث القدسية ومنزلتها في التشريع) .

Dr. W. A. Graham, (Divine Word and Prophetic Word in Early Islam), pp 95-101, Mouton, 1977.

33

٣ ـ التحلي بمكارم الأخلاق : والفضائل ، والبر ، وصلة الأرحام ، وحسن معاملة الخلق ، وحب الصالحين ، والأمر بالمعروف والنهي عن المنكر .

٤ ـ التفاني في سبيل الله : بالرضا بقضائه ، وحب لقائه ، وبذل النفس والنفيس في طاعته .

٥ ـ الاستعداد ليوم الحساب : وما فيه من ثواب وعقاب ، بدوام الاستغفار والتوبة ، والجمع بين الخشية والرجاء ، والتوسل إلى الله بصالح الأعمال وما يأذن به من شفاعة ، والثقة الكاملة في رحمة الله السابغة التي تسبق غضبه ، وتشمل عباده .

ومجمل القول في هذه الموضوعات أنها تجلّي معاني الألوهية والعبودية ، وتوضح أقداراً من أبعادهما . خاصة في المجالات الاعتقادية ، والتعبدية ، والسلوكية ، وهي لا تكاد تتجاوز هذه الدائرة إلى موضوعات التشريع ، أو الأحكام ، أو المعاملات ، التي تُعالج في مواضعها من مصادر الدين الأخرى من قرآن وحديث .

وأسلوب الأحاديث القدسية يناسب مضامينها وموضوعاتها . ويمكن وصفه بأنه يعتمد كثيراً على التعبير المباشر : إنْ بالنداء القدسي عن الله تعالى إلى عباده ، وإنْ بالمناجاة بينه وبينهم بقصد الإرشاد والهداية ، أو بغير ذلك من صور التعبير التي تعمق الصلة بين الخالق عز وجل وبين عباده . وأسلوب الأحاديث في جميع صورها علوي الطابع ، روحي الصبغة ، عميق الإثارة .

ولعل هذا هو أحد الأسباب التي جعلت مؤلفي كتب الترغيب والترهيب والرياضات الروحية والسلوكية ، يكثرون من الاستشهاد

بالأحاديث القدسية . إلا أن بعضهم قد توسع في ذلك بغير تحقيق كافٍ ، فوقع في كتبهم الضعيف وربما الموضوع ، وقد كان لهم في الصحيح والحسن من هذه الأحاديث مندوحة عن ذلك .

هذه المجموعة :

شهدت سنوات العقد الأخير عناية طيبة بتراثنا من الأحاديث القدسية : سواء بجمعها واستخراجها مباشرة من أمهات كتب الحديث كما ذكرنا آنفاً ، أم بإعادة نشر بعض ما نفد من المجموعات القديمة ، أم بإجراء دراسات حول الأحاديث وبيان حُجِّيتها وفقهها وما تضمنته من هداية وتوجيه ، أم بترجمة معانيها إلى اللغات الأخرى لتيسير الاطلاع عليها والإفادة منها من قبل الذين لا يعرفون العربية . ومع ذلك ، فإن الحاجة ما زالت قائمة لمزيد من العناية بهذا التراث ، من حيث الجمع ، والتحقيق ، والنشر ، والدراسة ، والترجمة .

لذلك فكرنا في إخراج هذه المجموعة مع ترجمة معانيها إلى اللغة الإنجليزية . وقد راعينا في اختيار الأحاديث التي تشتمل عليها هذه المجموعة ما يلي :

١ ـ أن يقتصر عددها على أربعين : مجاراة لما اتبعه مؤلفو المختارات المختصرة في الأحاديث ، من الاقتصار على هذا العدد ، استهداءً بقول النبي ﷺ « مَنْ حَفِظَ على أُمَّتي أَرْبَعِينَ حَدِيثاً مِنْ أَمْرِ دِينِها ، بَعَثَهُ اللَّهُ يَوْمَ القِيامةِ في زُمْرةِ الفُقَهَاءِ والعُلَمَاءِ »[1] ،

---

[1] انظر في وجه الاستشهاد بهذا الحديث ، ومدى حجيته ، ما ذكره النووي في مقدمة (الأربعين النووية) .

واقتناعاً بأن العدد المحدود يسهل الأمر على الدارسين ، ويشجعهم من بعد على الاستزادة ، وإذا وفّق الله في الاختيار فمن الممكن أن يضم ما يكفي من أصول التراث .

٢ ـ أن نلتزم بالتدقيق فيما نختار ، فلا نورد في هذه المجموعة إلا الصحيح والحسن . فمما اخترناه أربعة وثلاثون حديثاً مما اتفق عليه البخاري ومسلم في صحيحيهما ، أو ورد في أحدهما . أما الأحاديث الستة الباقية فمما ورد في كتب الأصول الأخرى بتصحيح أو تحسين ظاهرين ، وحرصنا على بيان ذلك في مواضعه . وعند ورود الحديث في أكثر من مصدر ، كما هي الحال مع معظم الأحاديث ، قدمنا المصدر الذي أخذنا روايته ، وذكرنا المصادر الأخرى بعده .

٣ ـ أن تكون الأحاديث صريحة الاتصاف بالقدسية ، إما بكونها قدسية النص من أول الحديث إلى آخره ، وإما باحتوائها على عبارة قدسية في السياق .

٤ ـ أن تمثل المجموعة المختارة معظم الموضوعات التي تناولتها الأحاديث القدسية ، بحيث يتمكن قارئها من الإحاطة بما اشتمل عليه عامة هذا التراث من هَدْي وما اتسم به من طابع . وقد أوردنا الأحاديث في المجموعة مرتبة وفقاً لتتابع الموضوعات مبتدئين بأحاديث العقيدة ، فالعبادات ، ففضائل الأخلاق والأعمال ، فالاستشهاد والصبر على قضاء الله ، فالاستغفار والتوبة ، وأخيراً أحاديث يوم الحساب . وجعلنا مفتتح الكتاب وآخره من أحاديث البشارات برحمة الله ورضوانه .

أما ترجمة معاني الأحاديث إلى اللغة الإنجليزية ، فقد اتجهنا

إليها ، متابعة لصنيعنا مع مجموعة الأحاديث النبوية التي اختارها الإمام النووي رحمه الله تعالى ، والمشهورة باسم (الأربعين النووية) . كما شجعنا على ذلك قلة ما ظهر حتى الآن من ترجمات لمعاني الأحاديث القدسية إلى اللغة الإنجليزية . إذ لا نعرف من ذلك إلا كتابيْن :

١ ـ «Hadees-e-Qudsi» ـ الحديث القدسي ـ وهي مجموعة من الأحاديث القدسية ، اختارها مولانا أحمد سعيد دهلوي ، وترجمها محمد سلمان إلى الإنجليزية نقلاً عن ترجمة أخرى بالأوردية . وقد طبع هذا الكتاب في الهند سنة ١٩٧٢ م ثم في سنة ١٩٧٦م ، محتوياً على الترجمة الإنجليزية وحدها . وأصول الأحاديث المترجمة متفاوتة الصحة ، وتشتمل على الضعيف ، وترجمتها في حاجة إلى إعادة نظر .

٢ ـ القسم الثالث من كتاب الدكتور وليام جراهام (Divine Word and Prophetic Word in Early Islam) ويشتمل على تسعين حديثاً بنصوصها ، وترجماتها . والنصوص أيضاً متفاوتة الصحة ، ولكنها معزوة إلى مصادرها بوضوح . وظهر هذا الكتاب في أمريكا سنة ١٩٧٧ .

وقد اتبعنا في ترجمة معاني هذه المجموعة إلى اللغة الإنجليزية ، نفس الطريقة التي اتبعت في ترجمة المجموعة السابقة (الأربعين النووية) . وهي أن يتشارك في الترجمة اثنان أحدهما عربي والثاني إنجليزي ، يتعاونان فيما بينهما ، ويكمل أحدهما جهد الآخر . وقد ساعدنا هذا التعاون على الاجتهاد في تحري الدقة والضبط في نقل

المعاني من أصولها العربية بلا اعتساف أو تصرف ، معتمدين في ذلك على الشروح الموثَّقة لها ، مع الحرص على صحة العبارة الإنجليزية واستقامتها وخلوها من التعقيد .

والتزمنا في ترجمة معاني الأحاديث حرفية النص . فإذا اضطررنا إلى التصرف الطفيف نبهنا إلى ذلك صراحة في الهامش ، وإذا احتيج إلى إضافة كلمة للإيضاح وضعناها بين معقوفين ، وأبقينا لفظ الجلالة على صيغته العربية دون ترجمة ، وكذلك بعض المصطلحات الدينية مثل : زكاة ، وذكر .

وفي الطباعة جمعنا بين النص العربي والترجمة الانجليزية متواجهيْن ، لتسهيل المراجعة . ولـم نورد من التعليقـات والملاحظـات الهامشية إلا ما اقتضته ضرورة واضحة إيثاراً للاختصار .

وغاية ما نرجوه أن نكون قد وفقنا في تزويد قارىء العربية بمجموعة موثقة من الأحاديث القدسية ، التي تقرب إليه هذا التراث ، وتحببه في الاستزادة منه ، وأن نكون كذلك قد يسرنا الأمر على قراء اللغة الانجليزية من المسلمين وغيرهم .

والله المسؤول أن يجعل عملنا هذا خالصاً لوجهه الكريم ، وأن يوفقنا لاستكمال ما وعدنا به من ترجمات مماثلة في حقل السنة النبوية الشريفة .

وآخر دعوانا أن الحمد لله رب العالمين .

أبو ظبي في غرة المحرم سنة ١٤٠٠ هـ
٢٠ نوفمبر سنة ١٩٧٩ م

عز الدين إبراهيم   دنيس جونسون ديفيز (عبد الودود)

HADITH 1

On the authority of Abū Hurayrah (may Allah be pleased with him), who said that the Messenger of Allah (may the blessings and peace of Allah be upon him) said:

When Allah decreed the Creation He pledged Himself by writing in His book which is laid down with Him: My mercy prevails over My wrath.

It was related by Muslim (also by al-Bukhārī, an-Nasāʾī and Ibn Mājah).

✻ ✻ ✻

الحديث الأول

عَنْ أبي هُرَيْرَةَ رَضِيَ اللهُ عنه ، قَالَ قَالَ رَسُولُ اللهِ صَلَّى اللهُ عليهِ وسلَّمَ :

« لَمَّا قَضَى اللَّهُ الخَلْقَ ، كَتَبَ في كِتَابِهِ على نَفْسِهِ ، فَهُوَ مَوْضُوعٌ عِنْدَهُ : إنَّ رَحْمَتِي تَغْلِبُ غَضَبِي » .

رَوَاهُ مُسْلِمٌ (وكذلِك البُخَارِيُّ وَالنَّسَائِيُّ وابْنُ مَاجَهْ) .

***

HADITH 2

On the authority of Abū Hurayrah (may Allah be pleased with him) from the Prophet (may the blessings and peace of Allah be upon him), who said: Allah the Almighty has said:

> The son of Adam denied Me and he had no right to do so. And he reviled Me and he had no right to do so. As for his denying Me, it is his saying: He will not remake me as He made me at first[1] – and the initial creation [of him] is no easier for Me than remaking him. As for his reviling Me, it is his saying: Allah has taken to Himself a son, while I am the One, the Everlasting Refuge. I begot not nor was I begotten, and there is none comparable to Me.

It was related by al-Bukhārī (also by an-Nasāʾī).

※ ※ ※

---

1. i.e. bring me back to life after death.

الحديث الثاني

عَنْ أَبِي هُرَيْرَةَ رَضِيَ اللَّهُ عَنْهُ، عَنِ النَّبِيِّ صَلَّى اللَّهُ عَلَيْهِ وَسَلَّمَ قَالَ:

« قَالَ اللَّهُ تَعَالَى: كَذَّبَنِي ابْنُ آدَمَ، وَلَمْ يَكُنْ لَهُ ذَلِكَ، وَشَتَمَنِي وَلَمْ يَكُنْ لَهُ ذَلِكَ. فَأَمَّا تَكْذِيبُهُ إِيَّايَ، فَقَوْلُهُ: لَنْ يُعِيدَنِي كَمَا بَدَأَنِي، وَلَيْسَ أَوَّلُ الْخَلْقِ بِأَهْوَنَ عَلَيَّ مِنْ إِعَادَتِهِ. وَأَمَّا شَتْمُهُ إِيَّايَ، فَقَوْلُهُ: اتَّخَذَ اللَّهُ وَلَدًا، وَأَنَا الْأَحَدُ الصَّمَدُ، لَمْ أَلِدْ وَلَمْ أُولَدْ، وَلَمْ يَكُنْ لِي كُفُوًا أَحَدٌ ».

رواه البخاري (وكذلك النسائي).

* * *

HADITH 3

On the authority of Zayd ibn Khālid al-Juhaniyy (may Allah be pleased with him), who said:

The Messenger of Allah (may the blessings and peace of Allah be upon him) led the morning prayer for us at al-Hudaybiyah following rainfall during the night. When the Prophet (may the blessings and peace of Allah be upon him) finished[1], he faced the people and said to them:

Do you know what your Lord has said? They said: Allah and His Messenger know best. He said: This morning one of My servants became a believer in Me and one a disbeliever. As for him who said: We have been given rain by virtue of Allah and His mercy, that one is a believer in Me, a disbeliever in the stars[2]; and as for him who said: We have been given rain by

---
1. Lit."left".
2. The pre-Islamic Arabs believed that rain was brought about by movements of the stars. This Hadith draws attention to the fact that whatever be the direct causes of such natural phenomena as rain, it is Allah the Almighty who is the Disposer of all things.

الحديث الثالث

عَنْ زَيْدِ بْنِ خَالِدٍ الجُهَنِّي، رَضِيَ اللَّهُ عَنْهُ قَالَ:

صَلَّى لَنَا رَسُولُ اللَّهِ، صَلَّى اللَّهُ عَلَيْهِ وَسَلَّمَ، صَلَاةَ الصُّبْحِ بِالْحُدَيْبِيَةِ، عَلَى إِثْرِ سَمَاءٍ⁽¹⁾ كَانَتْ مِنَ اللَّيْلَةِ. فَلَمَّا انْصَرَفَ النَّبِيُّ، صَلَّى اللَّهُ عَلَيْهِ وَسَلَّمَ، أَقْبَلَ عَلَى النَّاسِ، فَقَالَ لَهُمْ: «هَلْ تَدْرُونَ مَاذَا قَالَ رَبُّكُمْ؟ قَالُوا: اللَّهُ وَرَسُولُهُ أَعْلَمُ، قَالَ: أَصْبَحَ مِنْ عِبَادِي مُؤْمِنٌ بِي وَكَافِرٌ، فَأَمَّا مَنْ قَالَ: مُطِرْنَا بِفَضْلِ اللَّهِ وَرَحْمَتِهِ، فَذَلِكَ مُؤْمِنٌ بِي، كَافِرٌ بِالْكَوْكَبِ. وَأَمَّا مَنْ قَالَ: مُطِرْنَا

---

(1) عقب مطر.

such-and-such a star, that one is a disbeliever in Me, a believer in the stars.

It was related by al-Bukhārī (also by Mālik and an-Nasā'ī).

✾ ✾ ✾

بِنَوْءِ^(١) كَذَا وَكَذَا ، فَذَلِكَ كَافِرٌ بِي ، مُؤْمِنٌ بِالكَوْكَبِ » .

رواه البخاري (وكذلك مالك والنسائي) .

* * *

---

(١) النوء : الكوكب ؛ ربطوا نزول المطر به . والله خالق الكوكب ومُسيِّرٌ لكل الظواهر الطبيعية .

HADITH 4

On the authority of Abū Hurayrah (may Allah be pleased with him), who said that the Messenger of Allah (may the blessings and peace of Allah be upon him) said: Allah said:

> Sons of Adam inveigh against [the vicissitudes of] Time, and I am Time, in My hand is the night and the day¹.

It was related by al-Bukhārī (also by Muslim).

❈ ❈ ❈

---

1. As the Almighty is the Ordainer of all things, to inveigh against misfortunes that are part of Time is tantamount to inveighing against Him.

الحديث الرابع

عَنْ أبي هُرَيْرَةَ، رَضِيَ اللهُ عَنْهُ، قَالَ: قَالَ رَسُولُ اللهِ صَلَّى اللهُ عَلَيْهِ وَسَلَّمَ:

« قَالَ اللَّهُ: يَسُبُّ بَنُو آدَمَ الدَّهْرَ، وَأَنَا الدَّهْرُ، بِيَدِي اللَّيْلُ وَالنَّهَارُ ».

رواه البخاري (وكذلك مسلم) .

* * *

HADITH 5

On the authority of Abū Hurayrah (may Allah be pleased with him), who said that the Messenger of Allah (may the blessings and peace of Allah be upon him) said: Allah (glorified and exalted be He) said:

> I am so self-sufficient that I am in no need of having an associate[1]. Thus he who does an action for someone else's sake as well as Mine will have that action renounced by Me to him whom he associated with Me.

It was related by Muslim (also by Ibn Mājah).

✳ ✳ ✳

---

1. Lit. "I am the most self-sufficient of associates and am in no need of having an associate."

الحديث الخامس

عَنْ أَبِي هُرَيْرَةَ، رَضِيَ اللَّهُ عَنْهُ، قَالَ: قَالَ رَسُولُ اللَّهِ صَلَّى اللَّهُ عَلَيْهِ وَسَلَّمَ:

« قَالَ اللَّهُ تَبَارَكَ وَتَعَالَى: أَنَا أَغْنَى الشُّرَكَاءِ عَنِ الشِّرْكِ؛ مَنْ عَمِلَ عَمَلاً أَشْرَكَ فِيهِ غَيْرِي(1)، تَرَكْتُهُ وَشِرْكَهُ ».

رواه مسلم (وكذلك ابن ماجَهْ) .

* * *

---

(1) أشرك في قصده إذ عمل العمل لله ولغيره .

HADITH 6

On the authority of Abū Hurayrah (may Allah be pleased with him), who said: I heard the Messenger of Allah (may the blessings and peace of Allah be upon him) say:

The first of people against whom judgment will be pronounced on the Day of Resurrection will be a man who has died a martyr. He will be brought and Allah will make known to him His favours and he will recognise them. [The Almighty] will say: And what did you do about them? He will say: I fought for You until I died a martyr. He will say: You have lied — you did but fight that it might be said [of you]: He is courageous. And so it was said. Then he will be ordered to be dragged along on his face until he is cast into Hell-fire.

[Another] will be a man who has studied [religious] knowledge and has taught it and who used to recite the Qurʾān. He will be brought and Allah will make known to him His favours and he will recognise them. [The Almighty] will say: And what did you do about them? He will say: I studied [religious] knowledge and I taught it

الحديث السادس

عَنْ أبي هُرَيْرَةَ، رَضِيَ اللَّهُ عَنْهُ، قَالَ: سَمِعْتُ رَسُولَ اللَّهِ صَلَّى اللَّهُ عَلَيْهِ وَسَلَّمَ يَقُولُ:

« إِنَّ أَوَّلَ النَّاسِ يُقْضَى يَوْمَ القِيَامَةِ عَلَيْهِ رَجُلٌ اسْتُشْهِدَ، فَأُتِيَ بِهِ فَعَرَّفَهُ نِعَمَهُ فَعَرَفَهَا. قَالَ: فَمَا عَمِلْتَ فِيهَا؟ قَالَ قَاتَلْتُ فِيكَ حَتَّى اسْتُشْهِدْتُ، قَالَ: كَذَبْتَ، وَلٰكِنَّكَ قَاتَلْتَ لِأَنْ يُقَالَ: جَرِيءٌ، فَقَدْ قِيلَ. ثُمَّ أُمِرَ بِهِ فَسُحِبَ عَلَى وَجْهِهِ حَتَّى أُلْقِيَ فِي النَّارِ. وَرَجُلٌ تَعَلَّمَ العِلْمَ وَعَلَّمَهُ وَقَرَأَ القُرْآنَ، فَأُتِيَ بِهِ، فَعَرَّفَهُ نِعَمَهُ فَعَرَفَهَا. قَالَ: فَمَا عَمِلْتَ فِيهَا؟ قَالَ: تَعَلَّمْتُ العِلْمَ وَعَلَّمْتُهُ، وَقَرَأْتُ فِيكَ

and I recited the Qur'ān for Your sake. He will say: You have lied — you did but study [religious] knowledge that it might be said [of you]: He is learned. And you recited the Qur'ān that it might be said [of you]: He is a reciter. And so it was said. Then he will be ordered to be dragged along on his face until he is cast into Hell-fire.

[Another] will be a man whom Allah had made rich and to whom He had given all kinds of wealth. He will be brought and Allah will make known to him His favours and he will recognise them. [The Almighty] will say: And what did you do about them? He will say: I left no path [untrodden] in which You like money to be spent without spending in it for Your sake. He will say: You have lied—you did but do so that it might be said [of you]: He is open-handed. And so it was said. Then he will be ordered to be dragged along on his face until he is cast into Hell-fire.

It was related by Muslim (also by at-Tirmidhī and an-Nasā'ī).

القُرآنَ ، قَالَ : كَذَبْتَ ، ولٰكِنَّكَ تَعَلَّمْتَ العِلمَ لِيُقالَ : عالِمٌ ، وقَرأتَ القُرآنَ ، لِيُقالَ : هُوَ قارِيءٌ ، فقدْ قِيلَ ، ثُمَّ أُمِرَ بِهِ ، فَسُحِبَ عَلى وَجْهِهِ ، حَتَّى أُلْقِيَ فِي النَّارِ. ورَجُلٌ وَسَّعَ اللَّهُ عَلَيْهِ ، وَأَعْطَاهُ مِنْ أصنافِ المالِ كُلِّهِ ، فَأُتِيَ بِهِ ، فَعَرَّفَهُ نِعَمَهُ فَعَرَفَها . قَالَ : فَمَا عَمِلْتَ فِيها ؟ قَالَ : مَا تَرَكْتُ مِنْ سَبِيلٍ تُحِبُّ أَنْ يُنْفَقَ فِيها إلَّا أَنْفَقْتُ فِيها لَكَ ، قَالَ : كَذَبْتَ ، وَلٰكِنَّكَ فَعَلْتَ لِيُقالَ : هُوَ جَوادٌ ، فقدْ قِيلَ ، ثمَّ أُمِرَ بِهِ ، فَسُحِبَ عَلَى وَجْهِهِ ، ثُـمَّ أُلْقِيَ فِي النَّارِ» .

رواه مسلم (وكذلك الترمذي والنسائي) .

※ ※ ※

HADITH 7

On the authority of ᶜUqbah ibn ᶜĀmir (may Allah be pleased with him), who said: I heard the Messenger of Allah (may the blessings and peace of Allah be upon him) say:

> Your Lord delights at a shepherd who, on the peak of a mountain crag, gives the call to prayer and prays. Then Allah (glorified and exalted be He) says: Look at this servant of Mine, he gives the call to prayer and performs the prayers; he is in awe of Me. I have forgiven My servant [his sins] and have admitted him to Paradise.

It was related by an-Nasāʾī with a good chain of authorities.

※ ※ ※

الحديثُ السَّابعُ

عَنْ عُقْبَةَ بنِ عَامرٍ، رَضِيَ اللهُ عَنْهُ، قَالَ: سَمِعْتُ رَسُولَ اللهِ صَلَّى اللهُ عَلَيْهِ وَسَلَّمَ، يَقُولُ:

« يَعْجَبُ رَبُّكَ مِنْ رَاعِي غَنَمٍ، في رَأْسِ شَظِيَةِ الجَبَلِ(١)، يُؤَذِّنُ بالصَّلاةِ وَيُصَلِّي. فَيقُولُ اللهُ، عَزَّ وَجَلَّ،: انظُروا إلى عَبْدِي هَذَا، يُؤَذِّنُ وَيُقيمُ الصَّلاةَ، يَخَافُ مِنِّي، قَدْ غَفَرْتُ لِعَبْدِي، وَأَدْخَلْتُهُ الجَنَّةَ ».

رواه النسائي بسند صحيح (٢).

***

---

(١) شَظِيَّةُ الجبل: فِلقة منه.
(٢) انظر الألباني: (مشكاة المصابيح). حديث ٦٦٥.

HADITH 8

On the authority of Abū Hurayrah (may Allah be pleased with him) from the Prophet (may the blessings and peace of Allah be upon him), who said:

A prayer performed by someone who has not recited the Essence of the Qurʾān[1] during it is deficient (and he repeated the word three times), incomplete. Someone said to Abū Hurayrah: [Even though] we are behind the imām?[2] He said: Recite it to yourself, for I have heard the Prophet (may the blessings and peace of Allah be upon him) say: Allah (mighty and sublime be He), has said:

I have divided prayer between Myself and My servant into two halves, and My servant shall have what he has asked for. When the servant says: **Al-ḥamdu lillāhi rabbi ʾl-ʿālamīn,**[3] Allah (mighty and sublime be He) says: My servant has praised Me. And when he says: **Ar-raḥmāni ʾr-raḥīm,**[4]

---

1. Sūrat al-Fātiḥah, the first sūrah of the Qurʾān.
2. i.e. standing behind the imām listening to him reciting al-Fātiḥah.
3. "Praise be to Allah, Lord of the worlds."
4. "The Merciful, the Compassionate."

الْحَديثُ الثَّامِنُ

عَنْ أَبي هُرَيْرَةَ ، رَضِيَ اللَّهُ عَنْهُ ، عَنِ النَّبِيِّ ، صَلَّى اللَّهُ عَلَيْهِ وَسَلَّمَ ، قَالَ :

« مَنْ صَلَّى صَلَاةً لَمْ يَقْرَأْ فِيهَا بِأُمِّ القُرْآنِ ، فَهِيَ خِدَاجٌ[1] ، ثَلَاثاً ، غَيْرُ تَمَامٍ . فَقِيلَ لِأَبِي هُرَيْرَةَ : إِنَّا نَكُونُ وَرَاءَ الإِمَامِ . فَقَالَ : اقْرَأْ بِهَا فِي نَفْسِكَ ، فَإِنِّي سَمِعْتُ النَّبِيَّ ، صَلَّى اللَّهُ عَلَيْهِ وَسَلَّمَ ، يَقُولُ : « قَالَ اللَّهُ عَزَّ وَجَلَّ : قَسَمْتُ الصَّلَاةَ بَيْنِي وَبَيْنَ عَبْدِي نِصْفَيْنِ ، وَلِعَبْدِي مَا سَأَلَ . فَإِذَا قَالَ العَبْدُ : ﴿الحَمْدُ لِلَّهِ رَبِّ العَالَمِينَ﴾ قَالَ اللَّهُ ، عَزَّ وَجَلَّ : حَمِدَنِي عَبْدِي ، وَإِذَا قَالَ : ﴿الرَّحْمَٰنِ الرَّحِيمِ﴾ قَالَ اللَّهُ عَزَّ وَجَلَّ :

---

[1] خِدَاجٌ : نَاقِصَةٌ ، مِنْ خَدَجَ إِذَا نَقَصَ .

Allah (mighty and sublime be He) says: My servant has extolled Me, and when he says: **Māliki yawmi ʾd-dīn,**[1] Allah says: My servant has glorified Me — and on one occasion He said: My servant has submitted to My power. And when he says: **Iyyāka naʿbudu wa iyyāka nastaʿīn**[2], He says: This is between Me and My servant, and My servant shall have what he has asked for. And when he says: **Ihdinā ʾs-sirāta ʾl-mustaqīm, sirāta ʾlladhīna anʿamta ʿalayhim ghayri ʾl-maghdūbi ʿalayhim wa lā ʾd-dāllīn,**[3] He says: This is for My servant, and My servant shall have what he has asked for.

It was related by Muslim (also by Mālik, at-Tirmidhī, Abū Dāwūd, an-Nasāʾī and Ibn Mājah).

---

1. "Master of the Day of Judgment."
2. "It is You we worship and it is You we ask for help."
3. "Guide us to the straight path, the path of those upon whom You have bestowed favours, not of those against whom You are angry, nor of those who are astray."

أثْنـى عَلَيَّ عَبْـدِي ، وإذا قَالَ : ﴿مَـالِكِ يَوْمِ الدِّينِ﴾ قَالَ اللهُ : مجَّدَني عَبْدِي ـ وقَالَ مَرَّةً : فَوَّضَ إِليَّ عَبْدِي ـ فإذا قَالَ : ﴿إيَّاكَ نَعْبُدُ وإيَّاكَ نَسْتَعينُ﴾ قَالَ : هذا بَيْني وبَيْنَ عَبْدِي ، ولِعَبْدِي مَا سَأَلَ . فإذا قَالَ : ﴿اهْدِنا الصِّراطَ المُسْتَقِيمَ صِراطَ الَّذينَ أَنْعَمْتَ عَلَيْهمْ غَيْرِ المَغْضُوبِ عَلَيْهمْ ولاَ الضَّالِّينَ﴾ قَالَ : هذا لِعَبْدِي ، ولِعَبْدِي مَا سَأَلَ » .

رواه مسلم (وكذلك مالك والترمذي وأبو داود والنسائي وابـن ماجه) .

***

HADITH 9

On the authority of Abū Hurayrah (may Allah be pleased with him), who said that the Messenger of Allah (may the blessings and peace of Allah be upon him) said:

The first of his actions[1] for which a servant of Allah will be held accountable on the Day of Resurrection will be his prayers. If they are in order, then he will have prospered and succeeded; and if they are wanting, then he will have failed and lost. If there is something defective in his obligatory prayers, the Lord (glorified and exalted be He) will say: See if My servant has any supererogatory prayers with which may be completed that which was defective in his obligatory prayers. Then the rest of his actions[1] will be judged in like fashion.

It was related by at-Tirmidhī (also by Abū Dāwūd, an-Nasāʾī, Ibn Mājah and Aḥmad).

---

1. i.e. in respect of his religious duties.

الحديث التاسع

عَنْ أَبِي هُرَيْرَةَ ، رَضِيَ اللَّهُ عَنْهُ ، قَالَ : قَالَ رَسُولُ اللَّهِ صَلَّى اللَّهُ عَلَيْهِ وَسَلَّمَ :

« إِنَّ أَوَّلَ مَا يُحَاسَبُ بِهِ الْعَبْدُ يَوْمَ الْقِيَامَةِ مِنْ عَمَلِهِ صَلَاتُهُ . فَإِنْ صَلَحَتْ فَقَدْ أَفْلَحَ وَأَنْجَحَ ، وَإِنْ فَسَدَتْ فَقَدْ خَابَ وَخَسِرَ . فَإِنِ انْتَقَصَ مِنْ فَرِيضَتِهِ شَيْءٌ ، قَالَ الرَّبُّ عَزَّ وَجَلَّ : انْظُرُوا هَلْ لِعَبْدِي مِنْ تَطَوُّعٍ فَيُكَمَّلَ بِهَا مَا انْتَقَصَ مِنَ الْفَرِيضَةِ . ثُمَّ يَكُونُ سَائِرُ عَمَلِهِ عَلَى ذَلِكَ » .

رواه الترمذي[1] (وكذلك أبو داود والنسائي وابن ماجه وأحمد) .

---

[1] انظر أحمد شاكر :(سنن الترمذي) حديث ٤١٣ - ج ٢ ص ٢٧١ حيث يبين تحسينه . وانظر الألباني :(مشكاة المصابيح)- حديث ١٣٣٠ - ١٣٣١ ج ١ ص ٤١٩ حيث يصححه .

HADITH 10

On the authority of Abū Hurayrah (may Allah be pleased with him) from the Prophet (may the blessings and peace of Allah be upon him), who said: Allah (mighty and sublime be He) says:

> Fasting is Mine and it is I who give reward for it. [A man] gives up his sexual passion, his food and his drink for My sake. Fasting is like a shield, and he who fasts has two joys: a joy when he breaks his fast and a joy when he meets his Lord. The change in the breath[1] of the mouth of him who fasts is better in Allah's estimation than the smell of musk.

It was related by al-Bukhārī (also by Muslim, Mālik, at-Tirmidhī, an-Nasāʾī and Ibn Mājah).

* * *

---

1. As fasting may cause bad breath, the Hadith is an assurance that this fact should not discourage a Muslim from fasting.

الحديث العاشر

عَنْ أبي هُرَيْرَةَ، رَضِيَ اللَّهُ عَنْهُ، عَنِ النَّبِيِّ، صَلَّى اللَّهُ عَلَيْهِ وَسَلَّمَ، قَالَ:

« يَقُولُ اللَّهُ عَزَّ وَجَلَّ: الصَّوْمُ لِي، وَأَنَا أَجْزِي بِهِ، يَدَعُ شَهْوَتَهُ وَأَكْلَهُ وَشُرْبَهُ مِنْ أَجْلِي، والصَّوْمُ جُنَّةٌ(١)، وَلِلصَّائِمِ فَرْحَتَانِ: فَرْحَةٌ حِينَ يُفْطِرُ، وَفَرْحَةٌ حِينَ يَلْقَى رَبَّهُ، وَلَخُلُوفُ(٢) فَمِ الصَّائِمِ أَطْيَبُ عِنْدَ اللَّهِ مِنْ رِيحِ المِسْكِ ».

رواه البخاري (وكذلك مسلم ومالك والترمذي والنسائي وابن ماجه).

* * *

(١) الصوم جُنَّة: أي وقاية.
(٢) الخلوف: تغيّر الطعم والرائحة.

HADITH 11

On the authority of Abū Hurayrah (may Allah be pleased with him), who said that the Messenger of Allah (may the blessings and peace of Allah be upon him) said: Allah said:

Spend[1], O son of Adam, and I shall spend on you.

It was related by al-Bukhārī (also by Muslim).

❋ ❋ ❋

---

1. i.e. on charity.

الحديث الحادي عشر

عَنْ أَبِي هُرَيْرَةَ ، رَضِيَ اللَّهُ عَنْهُ ، أَنَّ رَسُولَ اللَّهِ صَلَّى اللَّهُ عَلَيْهِ وَسَلَّمَ قَالَ :

« قَالَ اللَّهُ : أَنْفِقْ يَا ابْنَ آدَمَ ، أُنْفِقْ عَلَيْكَ » .

رواه البخاري (وكذلك مسلم) .

* * *

HADITH 12

On the authority of Abū Mas`ūd al-Anṣārī (may Allah be pleased with him), who said that the Messenger of Allah (may the blessings and peace of Allah be upon him) said:

A man from among those who were before you was called to account. Nothing in the way of good was found for him except that he used to have dealings with[1] people and, being well-to-do, he would order his servants to let off the man in straitened circumstances [from repaying his debt]. He[2] said that Allah said: We are worthier than you of that[3]. Let him off.

It was related by Muslim (also by al-Bukhārī and an-Nasā'ī).

---

1. Lit. "mixed with".
2. i.e. the Prophet.
3. i.e. of being so generous.

الحديث الثاني عشر

عَنْ أَبِي مَسْعُودٍ الأَنْصَارِيِّ، رَضِيَ اللَّهُ عَنْهُ، قَالَ: قَالَ رَسُولُ اللَّهِ صَلَّى اللَّهُ عَلَيْهِ وسَلَّم:

« حُوسِبَ رَجُلٌ مِمَّنْ كَانَ قَبْلَكُمْ، فَلَمْ يُوجَدْ لَهُ مِنَ الْخَيْرِ شَيْءٌ، إِلاَّ أَنَّهُ كَانَ يُخَالِطُ[1] النَّاسَ، وَكَانَ مُوسِراً، فَكَانَ يَأْمُرُ غِلْمَانَهُ أَنْ يَتَجَاوَزُوا عَنِ المُعْسِرِ. قَالَ[2]، قَالَ اللَّهُ: نَحْنُ أَحَقُّ بِذَلِكَ مِنْكَ. تَجَاوَزُوا عَنْهُ ».

رواه مسلم (وكذلك البخاري والنسائي).

---

(١) يخالط الناس: يتعامل مع الناس في المال ويشاركهم. وفي رواية « يُدايِنُ النَّاسَ » وهي توضح المقصود.
(٢) أي الرسول ﷺ.

69

HADITH 13

On the authority of ᶜAdiyy ibn Ḥātim (may Allah be pleased with him), who said:

I was with the Messenger of Allah (may the blessings and peace of Allah be upon him) and there came to him two men: one of them was complaining of penury, while the other was complaining of brigandry. The Messenger of Allah (may the blessings and peace of Allah be upon him) said: As for brigandry, it will be but a short time before a caravan will [be able to] go out to Mecca without a guard. As for penury, the Hour[1] will not arrive before one of you takes his charity around without finding anyone to accept it from him.

Then[2] one of you will surely stand before Allah, there being no screen between Him and him, nor an interpreter to translate for him. Then He will say to him: Did I not bring you wealth? And he will say: Yes. Then He

---
1. i.e. of the Day of Judgment.
2. i.e. at the time of the Hour.

الحديث الثالث عشر

عَنْ عَدِيَّ بْنِ حَاتِمٍ ، رَضِيَ اللَّهُ عَنْهُ ، يَقُولُ :

« كُنْتُ عِنْدَ رَسُولِ اللَّهِ ، صَلَّى اللَّهُ عَلَيْهِ وَسَلَّمَ ، فَجَاءَهُ رَجُلَانِ : أَحَدُهُمَا يَشْكُو الْعَيْلَةَ(1) ، وَالآخَرُ يَشْكُو قَطْعَ السَّبِيلِ(2) ، فَقَالَ رَسُولُ اللَّهِ ، صَلَّى اللَّهُ عَلَيْهِ وَسَلَّمَ : أَمَّا قَطْعُ السَّبِيلِ فَإِنَّهُ لَا يَأْتِي عَلَيْكَ إِلَّا قَلِيلٌ ، حَتَّى تَخْرُجَ الْعِيرُ إِلَى مَكَّةَ بِغَيْرِ خَفِيرٍ . وَأَمَّا الْعَيْلَةُ ، فَإِنَّ السَّاعَةَ لَا تَقُومُ حَتَّى يَطُوفَ أَحَدُكُمْ بِصَدَقَتِهِ ، لَا يَجِدُ مَنْ يَقْبَلُهَا مِنْهُ . ثُمَّ لَيَقِفَنَّ أَحَدُكُمْ بَيْنَ يَدَيِ اللَّهِ ، لَيْسَ بَيْنَهُ وَبَيْنَهُ حِجَابٌ وَلَا تَرْجُمَانٌ يُتَرْجِمُ لَهُ ، ثُمَّ لَيَقُولَنَّ لَهُ : أَلَمْ أُوتِكَ مَالًا ؟ فَلَيَقُولَنَّ : بَلَى ، ثُمَّ لَيَقُولَنَّ : أَلَمْ أُرْسِلْ

---

(1) العَيْلة : الفقر والحاجة .
(2) قطع السبيل : التلصص في الطريق ، وإرعاب المارين والمسافرين .

will say: Did I not send to you a messenger? And he will say: Yes. And he will look to his right and will see nothing but Hell-fire, then he will look to his left and will see nothing but Hell-fire, so let each of you protect himself against Hell-fire, be it with even half a date — and if he finds it not, then with a kind word.

It was related by al-Bukhārī.

※ ※ ※

إِلَيْكَ رَسُولاً ؟ فَلَيَقُولَنَّ : بَلَى . فَيَنْظُرُ عَنْ يَمِينِهِ ، فَلاَ يَرَى إِلاَّ النَّارَ ، ثُمَّ يَنْظُرُ عَنْ شِمَالِهِ ، فَلاَ يَرَى إِلاَّ النَّارَ . فَلْيَتَّقِيَنَّ أَحَدُكُمُ النَّارَ ، وَلَوْ بِشِقِّ تَمْرَةٍ ، فَإِنْ لَمْ يَجِدْ فَبِكَلِمَةٍ طَيِّبَةٍ » .

رواه البخاري .

* * *

HADITH 14

On the authority of Abū Hurayrah (may Allah be pleased with him) from the Prophet (may the blessings and peace of Allah be upon him), who said:

Allah (glorified and exalted be He) has supernumerary angels who rove about seeking out gatherings in which Allah's name is being invoked; they sit with them and fold their wings round each other, filling that which is between them and between the lowest heaven. When [the people in the gathering] depart, [the angels] ascend and rise up to heaven. He[1] said: Then Allah (mighty and sublime be He) asks them — [though] He is most knowing about them: From where have you come? And they say: We have come from some servants of Yours on earth: they were glorifying You[2], exalting You[3], witnessing that there is no god but You[4], praising You[5], and asking [favours] of You. He says: And what do

---

1. i.e. the Prophet.
2. i.e. by saying **Subhāna 'llāh** (How far is Allah from every imperfection).
3. i.e. by saying **Allāhu akbar** (Allah is most great).
4. i.e. by saying **Lā ilāha illā 'llāh** (There is no god but Allah).
5. i.e. by saying **Al-Hamdu lillah** (Praise be to Allah).

الحديث الرابع عشر

عَنْ أَبِي هُرَيْرَةَ ، رَضِيَ اللَّهُ عَنْهُ ، عَنِ النَّبِيِّ ، صَلَّى اللَّهُ عَلَيْهِ وَسَلَّمَ ، قَالَ :

« إِنَّ للهِ تَبَارَكَ وَتَعَالَى مَلَائِكَةً ، سَيَّارَةً فُضْلاً(١) ، يَبْتَغُونَ مَجَالِسَ الذِّكْرِ . فَإِذَا وَجَدُوا مَجْلِساً فِيهِ ذِكْرٌ ، قَعَدُوا مَعَهُمْ ، وَحَفَّ بَعْضُهُمْ بَعْضاً بِأَجْنِحَتِهِمْ ، حَتَّى يَمْلَأُوا مَا بَيْنَهُمْ وَبَيْنَ السَّمَاءِ الدُّنْيَا ، فَإِذَا انْصَرَفُوا عَرَجُوا وَصَعِدُوا إِلَى السَّمَاءِ . قَالَ(٢): فَيَسْأَلُهُمُ اللَّهُ ، عَزَّ وَجَلَّ، وَهُوَ أَعْلَمُ بِهِمْ : مِنْ أَيْنَ جِئْتُمْ ؟ فَيَقُولُونَ : جِئْنَا مِنْ عِنْدِ عِبَادٍ لَكَ فِي الأَرْضِ ، يُسَبِّحُونَكَ وَيُكَبِّرُونَكَ ، وَيُهَلِّلُونَكَ ، وَيَحْمَدُونَكَ ، وَيَسْأَلُونَكَ .

---

(١) فُضْلاً : جمع فاضل وهو الزائد ، فهم ملائكة زادهم الله وخصصهم لحِلَق الذكر .

(٢) أي الرسول صلى الله عليه وسلم .

they ask of Me? They say: They ask of You Your Paradise. He says: And have they seen My Paradise? They say: No, O Lord. He says: And how would it be were they to have seen My Paradise! They say: And they ask protection of You. He says: From what do they ask protection of Me? They say: From Your Hell-fire, O Lord. He says: And have they seen My Hell-fire? They say: No. He says: And how would it be were they to have seen My Hell-fire! They say: And they ask for Your forgiveness. He[1] said: Then He says: I have forgiven them and I have bestowed upon them what they have asked for, and I have granted them sanctuary from that from which they asked protection. He[1] said: They say: O Lord, among them is So--and-so, a much sinning servant, who was merely passing by and sat down with them. He[1] said: And He says: And to him [too] I have given forgiveness: he who sits with such people shall not suffer.

It was related by Muslim (also by al-Bukhārī, at-Tirmidhī and an-Nasāʾī).

---

1. i.e. the Prophet.

قَالَ : وَمَا يَسْأَلُونِي ؟ قَالُوا : يَسْأَلُونَكَ جَنَّتَكَ ، قَالَ : وَهَلْ رَأَوْا جَنَّتِي ؟ قَالُوا : لَا ، أَيْ رَبِّ ، قَالَ : فَكَيْفَ لَوْ رَأَوْا جَنَّتِي ! قَالُوا : وَيَسْتَجِيرُونَكَ ، قَالَ : وَمِمَّ يَسْتَجِيرُونِي ؟ قَالُوا : مِنْ نَارِكَ يَا رَبِّ ، قَالَ : وَهَلْ رَأَوْا نَارِي ؟ قَالُوا : لَا ، قَالَ : فَكَيْفَ لَوْ رَأَوْا نَارِي ! قَالُوا : وَيَسْتَغْفِرُونَكَ ، قَالَ[1] فَيَقُولُ : قَدْ غَفَرْتُ لَهُمْ ، وَأَعْطَيْتُهُمْ مَا سَأَلُوا ، وَأَجَرْتُهُمْ مِمَّا اسْتَجَارُوا . قَالَ[1] : يَقُولُونَ : رَبِّ فِيهِمْ فُلَانٌ ، عَبْدٌ خَطَّاءٌ ، إِنَّمَا مَرَّ فَجَلَسَ مَعَهُمْ . قَالَ[1] : فَيَقُولُ : وَلَهُ غَفَرْتُ ؛ هُمُ القَوْمُ ، لَا يَشْقَى بِهِمْ جَلِيسُهُمْ » .

رواه مسلم (وكذلك البخاري والترمذي والنسائي) .

---

(١) أي الرسول صلّى الله عليه وسلم .

HADITH 15

On the authority of Abū Hurayrah (may Allah be pleased with him), who said that the Prophet (may the blessings and peace of Allah be upon him) said: Allah the Almighty says:

I am as My servant thinks I am[1]. I am with him when he makes mention of Me. If he makes mention of Me to himself, I make mention of him to Myself; and if he makes mention of Me in an assembly, I make mention of him in an assembly better than it. And if he draws near to Me a hand's span, I draw near to him an arm's length; and if he draws near to Me an arm's length, I draw near to him a fathom's length. And if he comes to Me walking, I go to him at speed.

It was related by al-Bukhārī (also by Muslim, at-Tirmidhī and Ibn Mājah).

---

1. Another possible rendering of the Arabic is: "I am as My servant expects Me to be". The meaning is that forgiveness and acceptance of repentance by the Almighty is subject to His servant truly believing that He is forgiving and merciful. However, not to accompany such belief with right action would be to mock the Almighty.

الحديث الخامس عشر

عَنْ أبي هُرَيْرَةَ ، رَضِيَ اللهُ عَنْهُ ، قَالَ : قَالَ النَّبِيُّ ، صَلَّى اللهُ عَلَيْهِ وَسَلَّمَ :

« يَقُولُ اللهُ تَعَالَى : أنا عِنْدَ ظَنِّ عَبْدِي بِي ، وَأَنا مَعَهُ إِذا ذَكَرَنِي ، فَإِنْ ذَكَرَنِي فِي نَفْسِهِ ، ذَكَرْتُهُ فِي نَفْسِي . وَإِنْ ذَكَرَنِي فِي مَلَإٍ ، ذَكَرْتُهُ فِي مَلَإٍ خَيْرٍ مِنْهُم ، وَإِنْ تَقَرَّبَ إِلَيَّ بِشِبْرٍ ، تَقَرَّبْتُ إِلَيْهِ ذِرَاعاً ، وَإِنْ تَقَرَّبَ إِلَيَّ ذِرَاعاً ، تَقَرَّبْتُ إِلَيْهِ بَاعاً[1] ، وَإِنْ أَتَانِي يَمْشِي ، أَتَيْتُهُ هَرْوَلَةً » .

رواه البخاري (وكذلك مسلم والترمذي وابن ماجه) .

---

[1] الباع : بقدر انبساط الذراعين في جهتيهما .

HADITH 16

On the authority of the son of ʿAbbās (may Allah be pleased with them both), from the Messenger of Allah (may the blessings and peace of Allah be upon him), that among the sayings he related from his Lord (glorified and exalted be He) is that He said:

Allah has written down the good deeds and the bad ones. Then He explained it [by saying that] he who has intended a good deed and has not done it, Allah writes it down with Himself as a full good deed, but if he has intended it and has done it, Allah writes it down with Himself as from ten good deeds to seven hundred times, or many times over. But if he has intended a bad deed and has not done it, Allah writes it down with Himself as a full good deed, but if he has intended it and has done it, Allah writes it down as one bad deed.

It was related by al-Bukhārī and Muslim.

※ ※ ※

الحديث السادس عشر

عَنْ ابْنِ عَبَّاسٍ، رَضِيَ اللهُ عَنْهُمَا، عَنِ النَّبِيِّ صَلَّى اللهُ عَلَيْهِ وَسَلَّمَ، فِيمَا يَرْوِي عَنْ رَبِّهِ عَزَّ وَجَلَّ، قَالَ:

« إِنَّ اللهَ كَتَبَ الْحَسَنَاتِ وَالسَّيِّئَاتِ، ثُمَّ بَيَّنَ ذَلِكَ: فَمَنْ هَمَّ بِحَسَنَةٍ فَلَمْ يَعْمَلْهَا، كَتَبَهَا اللهُ لَهُ عِنْدَهُ حَسَنَةً كَامِلَةً، فَإِنْ هُوَ هَمَّ بِهَا فَعَمِلَهَا، كَتَبَهَا اللهُ لَهُ عِنْدَهُ عَشْرَ حَسَنَاتٍ، إِلَى سَبْعِمِائَةِ ضِعْفٍ، إِلَى أَضْعَافٍ كَثِيرَةٍ. وَمَنْ هَمَّ بِسَيِّئَةٍ فَلَمْ يَعْمَلْهَا، كَتَبَهَا اللهُ لَهُ عِنْدَهُ حَسَنَةً كَامِلَةً، فَإِنْ هُوَ هَمَّ بِهَا فَعَمِلَهَا، كَتَبَهَا اللهُ سَيِّئَةً وَاحِدَةً. »

رواه البخاري ومسلم.

* * *

HADITH 17

On the authority of Abū Dharr al-Ghifārī (may Allah be pleased with him) from the Prophet (may the blessings and peace of Allah be upon him) is that among the sayings he relates from his Lord (may He be glorified) is that He said:

O My servants, I have forbidden oppression for Myself and have made it forbidden amongst you, so do not oppress one another.

O My servants, all of you are astray except for those I have guided, so seek guidance of Me and I shall guide you. O My servants, all of you are hungry except for those I have fed, so seek food of Me and I shall feed you. O My servants, all of you are naked except for those I have clothed, so seek clothing of Me and I shall clothe you. O My servants, you sin by night and by day, and I forgive all sins, so seek forgiveness of Me and I shall forgive you.

O My servants, you will not attain harming Me so as to harm Me, and you will not attain benefitting Me so as to benefit Me. O My servants, were the

اَلْحَدِيثُ السَّابِعَ عَشَرَ

عَنْ أبي ذرٍ الغِفاريِّ ، رَضِيَ اللّهُ عَنْهُ ، عَنِ النَّبيِّ ، صَلَّى اللَّهُ عَلَيْهِ وَسَلَّمَ ، فيما يَرْويهِ عَنْ رَبِّهِ عَزَّ وَجَلَّ ، أنَّهُ قَالَ :

« يَا عِبَادِي : إِنِّي حَرَّمْتُ الظُّلْمَ عَلَى نَفْسِي وَجَعَلْتُهُ بَيْنَكُمْ مُحَرَّماً فَلاَ تَظَالَمُوا .

يَا عِبَادِي : كُلُّكُمْ ضَالٌّ إلا مَنْ هَدَيْتُهُ فَاسْتَهْدُوني أَهْدِكُمْ . يَا عِبَادي : كُلُّكُمْ جَائِعٌ إلاَّ مَنْ أَطْعَمْتُهُ فَاسْتَطْعِمُوني أُطْعِمْكُمْ . يا عبادي : كُلُّكُمْ عارٍ إلاَّ مَنْ كَسَوْتُهُ فَاسْتَكْسُوني أَكْسُكُمْ . يا عبادي : إنَّكُمْ تُخْطِئُونَ بِاللَّيْلِ والنَّهارِ ، وَأَنا أغْفِرُ الذُّنُوبَ جَمِيعاً ، فَاسْتَغْفِرُوني أغْفِرْ لَكُمْ .

يَا عِبَادي : إنَّكُمْ لَنْ تَبْلُغُوا ضُرِّي فَتَضُرُّوني ، وَلَنْ تَبْلُغُوا نَفْعي فَتَنْفَعُوني . يَا عِبادي : لَوْ أنَّ أوَّلَكُمْ وَآخِرَكُمْ وَإِنْسَكُمْ وَجِنَّكُمْ

first of you and the last of you, the human of you and the jinn of you to be as pious as the most pious heart of any one man of you, that would not increase My kingdom in anything. O My servants, were the first of you and the last of you, the human of you and the jinn of you to be as wicked as the most wicked heart of any one man of you, that would not decrease My kingdom in anything. O My servants, were the first of you and the last of you, the human of you and the jinn of you to rise up in one place and make a request of Me, and were I to give everyone what he requested, that would not decrease what I have, any more than a needle decreases the sea if put into it.[1]

O My servants, it is but your deeds that I reckon up for you and then recompense you for, so let him who finds good[2] praise Allah and let him

---

1. This refers to the minute amount of water adhering to a needle if dipped into the sea and withdrawn.
2. i.e. in the Hereafter.

كَانُوا عَلَى أَتْقَى قَلْبِ رَجُلٍ وَاحِدٍ مِنْكُم ، ما زَادَ ذَلِكَ فِي مُلْكِي شَيئاً . يا عِبادي : لَوْ أَنَّ أَوَّلَكُمْ وَآخِرَكُمْ وَإِنْسَكُمْ وَجِنَّكُمْ كَانُوا عَلَى أَفْجَرِ قَلْبِ رَجُلٍ وَاحِدٍ مِنْـكُمْ مَا نَقَصَ ذَلِكَ مِنْ مُلْـكِي شَيئاً . يا عِبَادي : لَوْ أَنَّ أَوَّلَكُمْ وآخِرَكُمْ وَإِنْسَكُمْ وَجِنَّـكُمْ قَامُـوا فِي صَعِيدٍ واحـدٍ ، فَسَأَلُونـي ، فَأَعْطَيْتُ كُلَّ وَاحِدٍ مَسْأَلَتَهُ ، مَا نَقَصَ ذَلِكَ مِمَّا عِنْدي إلاَّ كَمَا يَنْقُصُ المِخْيَطُ إذا أُدْخِلَ البَحْرَ .

يَا عِبَادي : إِنَّمَا هِيَ أَعْمَالُكُمْ أُحْصِيها لَكُمْ ، ثُمَّ أُوَفِّيكُمْ إيَّاها ، فَمَنْ وَجَدَ خَيْراً فَلْيَحْمَدِ اللَّهَ ،

who finds other than that blame no one but himself.

It was related by Muslim (also by at-Tirmidhī and Ibn Mājah).

※ ※ ※

ومَنْ وَجَد غَيْرَ ذَلِكَ فَلاَ يَلُومَنَّ إلا نَفْسَهُ » .

رواهُ مُسْلمٌ (وكذلك الترمذي وابن ماجَهْ) .

※ ※ ※

HADITH 18

On the authority of Abū Hurayrah (may Allah be pleased with him), who said that the Messenger of Allah (may the blessings and peace of Allah be upon him) said: Allah (mighty and sublime be He) will say on the Day of Resurrection:

O son of Adam, I fell ill and you visited Me not. He will say: O Lord, and how should I visit You when You are the Lord of the worlds? He will say: Did you not know that My servant So-and-so had fallen ill and you visited him not? Did you not know that had you visited him you would have found Me with him? O son of Adam, I asked you for food and you fed Me not. He will say: O Lord, and how should I feed You when You are the Lord of the worlds? He will say: Did you not know that My servant So-and-so asked you for food and you fed him not? Did you not know that had you fed him you would surely have found that[1] with Me? O son of Adam, I asked you to give Me to drink and you gave Me not to drink. He will say: O Lord, how should

---

1. i.e. the reward for so doing.

الحديث الثامن عشر

عَنْ أَبِي هُرَيْرَةَ، رَضِيَ اللَّهُ عَنْهُ، قَالَ: قَالَ رَسُولُ اللَّهِ، صَلَّى اللَّهُ عَلَيْهِ وَسَلَّمَ:

« إِنَّ اللَّهَ، عَزَّ وَجَلَّ، يَقُولُ يَوْمَ القِيَامَةِ: يَا ابْنَ آدَمَ، مَرِضْتُ فَلَمْ تَعُدْنِي (١)، قال: يَا رَبِّ، وَكَيْفَ أَعُودُكَ وَأَنْتَ رَبُّ العَالَمِينَ؟ قَالَ: أَمَا عَلِمْتَ أَنَّ عَبْدِي فُلَاناً مَرِضَ فَلَمْ تَعُدْهُ؟ أَمَا عَلِمْتَ أَنَّكَ لَوْ عُدْتَهُ لَوَجَدْتَنِي عِنْدَهُ. يَا ابْنَ آدَمَ: اسْتَطْعَمْتُكَ فَلَمْ تُطْعِمْنِي، قَالَ: يَا رَبِّ، وَكَيْفَ أُطْعِمُكَ وَأَنْتَ رَبُّ العَالَمِينَ؟ قَالَ: أَمَا عَلِمْتَ أَنَّهُ اسْتَطْعَمَكَ عَبْدِي فُلَانٌ، فَلَمْ تُطْعِمْهُ؟ أَمَا عَلِمْتَ أَنَّكَ لَوْ أَطْعَمْتَهُ لَوَجَدْتَ ذَلِكَ عِنْدِي. يَا ابْنَ آدَمَ: اسْتَسْقَيْتُكَ، فَلَمْ تَسْقِنِي، قَالَ: يَا رَبِّ، كَيْفَ أَسْقِيكَ وَأَنْتَ رَبُّ

---

(١) عيادة المريض زيارته.

I give You to drink when You are the Lord of the worlds? He will say: My servant So-and-so asked you to give him to drink and you gave him not to drink. Had you given him to drink you would have surely found that[1] with Me.

It was related by Muslim.

* * *

---
[1] i.e. the reward for so doing.

العَالَمِينَ ؟ قَالَ : اسْتَسْقَاكَ عَبْدِي فُلانٌ فَلَمْ تَسْقِهِ ، أَمَا إِنَّكَ لَوْ سَقَيْتَهُ لَوَجَدْتَ ذَلِكَ عِنْدِي » .

رواه مسلم .

* * *

HADITH 19

On the authority of Abu Hurayrah (may Allah be pleased with him), who said that the Messenger of Allah (may the blessings and peace of Allah be upon him) said that Allah (glorified and exalted be He) said:

> Pride is My cloak and greatness My robe, and he who competes with Me in respect of either of them I shall cast into Hell-fire.

It was related by Abū Dāwūd (also by Ibn Mājah and Aḥmad) with sound chains of authority.[1]

※ ※ ※

---

[1]. This Hadith also appears in Muslim in another version.

الحديث التاسع عشر

عَنْ أبي هُرَيْرَةَ، رَضِيَ اللَّهُ عَنْهُ، قَالَ: قَالَ رَسُولُ اللَّهِ صَلَّى اللَّهُ عَلَيْهِ وَسَلَّمَ:

«قَالَ اللَّهُ عَزَّ وَجَلَّ: الْكِبْرِيَاءُ رِدَائِي، وَالْعَظَمَةُ إِزَارِي، فَمَنْ نَازَعَنِي وَاحِداً مِنْهُما، قَذَفْتُهُ فِي النَّارِ».

رَوَاه أبو داود (وكذلك ابن ماجه وأحمد) بأسانيد صحيحة.(١)

❊ ❊ ❊

---

(١) والحديث عند مسلم أيضاً، بنحوه. وانظر ابن علان: (دليل الفالحين) جـ ٥ ص ٩٤، والألباني: (الأحاديث الصحيحة). حديث ٥٣١.

HADITH 20

On the authority of Abū Hurayrah (may Allah be pleased with him) that the Messenger of Allah (may the blessings and peace of Allah be upon him) said:

The gates of Paradise will be opened on Mondays and on Thursdays, and every servant [of Allah] who associates nothing with Allah will be forgiven, except for the man who has a grudge against his brother. [About them] it will be said: Delay these two until they are reconciled; delay these two until they are reconciled; delay these two until they are reconciled.

It was related by Muslim (also by Mālik and Abu Dāwūd).

❊ ❊ ❊

اَلْحَدِيثُ الْعِشْرُونَ

عَنْ أَبِي هُرَيْرَةَ ، رَضِيَ اللَّهُ عَنْهُ ، أَنَّ رَسُولَ اللَّهِ ، صَلَّى اللَّهُ عَلَيْهِ وَسَلَّمَ ، قَالَ :

« تُفْتَحُ أَبْوَابُ الْجَنَّةِ يَوْمَ الِاثْنَيْنِ ، وَيَوْمَ الْخَمِيسِ ، فَيُغْفَرُ لِكُلِّ عَبْدٍ لَا يُشْرِكُ بِاللَّهِ شَيْئًا ، إِلَّا رَجُلًا كَانَتْ بَيْنَهُ وَبَيْنَ أَخِيهِ شَحْنَاءُ ، فَيُقَالُ :[1] أَنْظِرُوا[2] هَذَيْنِ ، حَتَّى يَصْطَلِحَا ، أَنْظِرُوا هَذَيْنِ حَتَّى يَصْطَلِحَا ، أَنْظِرُوا هَذَيْنِ حَتَّى يَصْطَلِحَا » .

رواه مسلم (وكذلك مالك وأبو داود) .

***

---

(١) أي من قبل الله تعالى .
(٢) أنظروا : أجِّلوا وأخِّروا .

HADITH 21

On the authority of Abū Hurayrah (may Allah be pleased with him) from the Prophet (may the blessings and peace of Allah be upon him), who said that Allah the Almighty said:

There are three[1] whose adversary I shall be on the Day of Resurrection: a man who has given his word by Me and has broken it; a man who has sold a free man[2] and has consumed the price; and a man who has hired a workman, has exacted his due in full from him and has not given him his wage.

It was related by al-Bukhārī (also by Ibn Mājah and Aḥmad ibn Ḥanbal).

※ ※ ※

---

1. i.e. types of men.
2. i.e. a man who has made a slave of another and has sold him.

الحديثُ الحادي والعشرونَ

عَنْ أبي هُرَيْرَةَ، رَضِيَ اللهُ عَنْهُ، عَنِ النَّبِيِّ صَلَّى اللهُ عَلَيْهِ وَسَلَّمَ، قَالَ:

«قَالَ اللهُ تَعَالى: ثَلَاثَةٌ أَنَا خَصْمُهُمْ يَوْمَ الْقِيَامَةِ: رَجُلٌ، أَعْطَى بِي ثُمَّ غَدَرَ(1)، وَرَجُلٌ بَاعَ حُرًّا فَأَكَلَ ثَمَنَهُ، وَرَجُلٌ اسْتَأْجَرَ أجيراً فاسْتَوْفَى مِنْهُ وَلَمْ يُعْطِهِ أجْرَهُ».

رَوَاهُ البُخاريُّ (وكذلك ابن ماجه وأحمد).

***

---

(1) أي أعطى عهداً بالله ثم نقضه.

HADITH 22

On the authority of Abū Saʿīd (may Allah be pleased with him), who said that the Messenger of Allah (may the blessings and peace of Allah be upon him) said:

Let not any one of you belittle himself. They said: O Messenger of Allah, how can any one of us belittle himself? He said: He finds a matter concerning Allah about which he should say something, and he does not say [it], so Allah (mighty and sublime be He) says to him on the Day of Resurrection: What prevented you from saying something about such-and-such and such-and-such? He says: [It was] out of fear of people. Then He says: Rather it is I whom you should more properly fear.

It was related by Ibn Mājah with a sound chain of authorities.

※ ※ ※

الحديث الثاني والعشرون

عَنْ أَبِي سَعِيدٍ، رَضِيَ اللهُ عَنْهُ، قَالَ: قَالَ رَسُولُ اللهِ، صَلَّى اللهُ عَلَيْهِ وَسَلَّمَ:

« لَا يَحْقِرْ أَحَدُكُمْ نَفْسَهُ . قَالُوا : يَا رَسُولَ اللهِ، كَيْفَ يَحْقِرُ أَحَدُنَا نَفْسَهُ؟ قَالَ : يَرَى أَمْرَ اللهِ عَلَيْهِ فِيهِ مَقَالٌ، ثُمَّ لَا يَقُولُ فِيهِ، فَيَقُولُ اللهُ، عَزَّ وَجَلَّ، لَهُ يَوْمَ القِيَامَةِ : مَا مَنَعَكَ أَنْ تَقُولَ فِي كَذَا وَكَذَا؟ فَيَقُولُ : خَشْيَةَ النَّاسِ، فَيَقُولُ : فَإِيَّايَ كُنْتَ أَحَقَّ أَنْ تَخْشَى ».

رواه ابن ماجه بسند صحيح[1].

* * *

---

[1] انظر ابن ماجه : حديث ٤٠٠٨ .

HADITH 23

On the authority of Abū Hurayrah (may Allah be pleased with him), who said that the Messenger of Allah (may the blessings and peace of Allah be upon him) said: Allah will say on the Day of Resurrection:

> Where are those who love one another through My glory? Today I shall give them shade in My shade, it being a day when there is no shade but My shade.

It was related by al-Bukhārī (also by Mālik).

❋ ❋ ❋

الحَدِيثُ الثَّالِثُ وَالعِشْرُونَ

عَنْ أَبِي هُرَيْرَةَ، رَضِيَ اللَّهُ عَنْهُ، قَالَ: قَالَ رَسُولُ اللَّهِ، صَلَّى اللَّهُ عَلَيْهِ وسَلَّمَ:

« إِنَّ اللَّهَ يَقُولُ يَوْمَ القِيَامَةِ: أَيْنَ المُتَحَابُّونَ بِجَلَالِي؟ اليَوْمَ أُظِلُّهُمْ فِي ظِلِّي يَوْمَ لَا ظِلَّ إِلَّا ظِلِّي. »

رواه البخاري (وكذلك مالك) .

✻ ✻ ✻

HADITH 24

On the authority of Abū Hurayrah (may Allah be pleased with him), who said that the Messenger of Allah (may the blessings and peace of Allah be upon him) said:

If Allah has loved a servant [of His] He calls Gabriel (on whom be peace) and says: I love So-and-so, therefore love him. He said[1]: So Gabriel loves him. Then he[2] calls out in heaven, saying: Allah loves So-and-so, therefore love him. And the inhabitants of heaven love him. He[1] said: Then acceptance is established for him on earth. And if Allah has abhorred a servant [of His], He calls Gabriel and says: I abhor So-and-so, therefore abhor him. So Gabriel abhors him. Then he[2] calls out to the inhabitants of heaven: Allah abhors So-and-so, therefore abhor him. He[1] said: So they abhor him, and abhorrence is established for him on earth.

It was related by Muslim (also by al-Bukhārī, Mālik and at-Tirmidhī).

---

1. i.e. the Prophet.
2. i.e. Gabriel.

الحديث الرابع والعشرون

عَنْ أَبِي هُرَيْرَةَ، رَضِيَ اللهُ عَنْهُ، قَالَ: قَالَ رَسُولُ اللهِ، صَلَّى اللهُ عَلَيْهِ وسلَّمَ:

« إِنَّ اللهَ إِذا أَحَبَّ عَبْداً دَعَا جِبْرِيلَ، عَلَيْهِ السَّلَامُ، فَقَالَ: إِنِّي أُحِبُّ فُلَاناً فَأَحِبَّهُ. قَالَ: فَيُحِبُّهُ جِبْرِيلُ، ثُمَّ يُنَادِي فِي السَّمَاءِ فَيَقُولُ: إِنَّ اللهَ يُحِبُّ فُلَاناً فَأَحِبُّوهُ، فَيُحِبُّهُ أَهْلُ السَّمَاءِ. قَالَ: ثُمَّ يُوضَعُ لَهُ القَبُولُ فِي الأَرْضِ. وَإِذَا أَبْغَضَ اللهُ عَبْداً، دَعَا جِبْرِيلَ، فَيَقُولُ: إِنِّي أُبْغِضُ فُلَاناً فَأَبْغِضْهُ. فَيُبْغِضُهُ جِبْرِيلُ، ثُمَّ يُنَادِي فِي أَهْلِ السَّمَاءِ: إِنَّ اللهَ يُبْغِضُ فُلَاناً، فَأَبْغِضُوهُ. قَالَ: فَيُبْغِضُونَهُ، ثُمَّ تُوضَعُ لَهُ البَغْضَاءُ فِي الأرضِ. »

رواه مسلم (وكذلك البخاري ومالك والترمذي).

※ ※ ※

HADITH 25

On the authority of Abū Hurayrah (may Allah be pleased with him), who said that the Messenger of Allah (may the blessings and peace of Allah be upon him) said: Allah (mighty and sublime be He) said:

> Whosoever shows enmity to someone devoted to Me, I shall be at war with him. My servant draws not near to Me with anything more loved by Me than the religious duties I have enjoined upon him, and My servant continues to draw near to Me with supererogatory works so that I shall love him. When I love him I am his hearing with which he hears, his seeing with which he sees, his hand with which he strikes and his foot with which he walks. Were he to ask [something] of Me, I would surely give it to him, and were he to ask Me for refuge, I would surely grant him it. I do not hesitate about anything as much as I hesitate about [seizing] the soul of My faithful servant: he hates death and I hate hurting him.

It was related by al-Bukhārī.

* * *

الحديث الخامس والعشرون

عَنْ أَبِي هُرَيْرَةَ، رَضِيَ اللهُ عَنْهُ، قَالَ رَسُولُ اللهِ، صَلَّى اللهُ عَلَيْهِ وَسَلَّمَ:

« إِنَّ اللهَ، عَزَّ وَجَلَّ، قَالَ: مَنْ عَادَى لِي وَلِيّاً، فَقَدْ آذَنْتُهُ بِالحَرْبِ، وَمَا تَقَرَّبَ إِلَيَّ عَبْدِي بِشَيْءٍ أَحَبَّ إِلَيَّ مِمَّا افْتَرَضْتُ عَلَيْهِ. وَمَا يَزَالُ عَبْدِي يَتَقَرَّبُ إِلَيَّ بِالنَّوَافِلِ حَتَّى أُحِبَّهُ، فَإِذَا أَحْبَبْتُهُ، كُنْتُ سَمْعَهُ الَّذِي يَسْمَعُ بِهِ، وَبَصَرَهُ الَّذِي يُبْصِرُ بِهِ، وَيَدَهُ الَّتِي يَبْطِشُ بِهَا، وَرِجْلَهُ الَّتِي يَمْشِي بِهَا، وَإِنْ سَأَلَنِي لَأُعْطِيَنَّهُ، وَلَئِنِ اسْتَعَاذَنِي لَأُعِيذَنَّهُ. وَمَا تَرَدَّدْتُ عَنْ شَيْءٍ أَنَا فَاعِلُهُ تَرَدُّدِي عَنْ نَفْسِ عَبْدِي المُؤْمِنِ، يَكْرَهُ المَوْتَ، وَأَنَا أَكْرَهُ مَسَاءَتَهُ. »

رواه البخاري.

* * *

HADITH 26

On the authority of Abū Umāmah (may Allah be pleased with him) from the Prophet (may the blessings and peace of Allah be upon him), who said that Allah (mighty and sublime be He) said:

Truly of those devoted to Me the one I most favour is a believer who is of meagre means and much given to prayer, who has been particular in the worship of his Lord and has obeyed Him inwardly[1], who was obscure among people and not pointed out, and whose sustenance was just sufficient to provide for him yet he bore this patiently.

Then he[2] rapped with his hand and said: Death will have come early to him, his mourners will have been few, his estate scant.

It was related by at-Tirmidhī (also by Aḥmad ibn Ḥanbal and Ibn Mājah). Its chain of authorities is sound.

---

1. i.e. he has not been ostentatious in his obedience.
2. i.e. the Prophet.

الْحَدِيثُ السَّادِسُ وَالْعِشْرُونَ

عَنْ أَبِي أُمَامَةَ، رَضِيَ اللهُ عَنْهُ، عَنِ النَّبِيِّ صَلَّى اللهُ عَلَيْهِ وَسَلَّمَ، قَالَ:

« قَالَ اللهُ عَزَّ وَجَلَّ : إِنَّ أَغْبَطَ أَوْلِيَائِي عِنْدِي لَمُؤْمِنٌ، خَفِيفُ الحَاذِ[1]، ذُو حَظٍّ مِنَ الصَّلَاةِ، أَحْسَنَ عِبَادَةَ رَبِّهِ، وَأَطَاعَهُ فِي السِّرِّ، وَكَانَ غَامِضاً فِي النَّاسِ، لَا يُشَارُ إِلَيْهِ بِالْأَصَابِعِ، وَكَانَ رِزْقُهُ كَفَافاً فَصَبَرَ عَلَى ذَلِكَ. ثُمَّ نَفَضَ بِيَدِهِ[2]، ثُمَّ قَالَ: عُجِّلَتْ مَنِيَّتُهُ، قَلَّتْ بَوَاكِيهِ، قَلَّ تُرَاثُهُ »[3].

رَوَاهُ التِّرْمِذِيُّ (وَكَذَلِكَ أَحْمَدُ وَابْنُ مَاجَهْ) وَإِسْنَادُهُ حَسَنٌ[4].

---

[1] خفيف الحاذ : قليل المال والعيال.
[2] أي النبي صلى الله عليه وسلم.
[3] تراثه : ميراثه.
[4] انظر : إبراهيم عطوة عوض : (سنن الترمذي) حديث ٢٣٤٧ ـ جـ ٤ ص ٥٧٥.
محمد فؤاد عبد الباقي : (سنن ابن ماجه) حديث ٤١١٧ ـ جـ ٢ ص ١٣٧٨.
الألباني : (مشكاة المصابيح) حديث ٥٨١٩ ـ جـ ٢ ص ٦٥٤.

HADITH 27

On the authority of Masrūq, who said:

We asked (or I asked)[1] ᶜAbdullah (i.e. Ibn Masᶜūd) about this verse: **And do not regard those who have been killed in the cause of Allah as dead, rather are they alive with their Lord, being provided for**[2]. He said: We asked about that and he[3] said: Their souls are in the insides of green birds having lanterns suspended from the Throne, roaming freely in Paradise where they please, then taking shelter in those lanterns. So their Lord cast a glance at them[4] and said: Do you wish for anything? They said: What shall we wish for when we roam freely in Paradise where we please? And thus did He do to them three times. When they saw that they would not be spared from being asked [again], they said: O Lord, we would like for You to put back our souls into our bodies so that we

---
1. An alternative reading.
2. Qurʾān, Chapter 3, Verse 169.
3. i.e. the Prophet.
4. i.e. at those who had been killed in the cause of Allah.

الحديث السابع والعشرون

عَنْ مَسْرُوقٍ، قَالَ:

سَأَلْنا ـ أَوْ سَأَلْتُ عَبْدَ اللهِ (أَيْ ابْنَ مَسْعُودٍ) عَنْ هَذِهِ الآيةِ:

﴿ وَلاَ تَحْسَبَنَّ الَّذِينَ قُتِلُوا فِي سَبِيلِ اللهِ أَمْواتاً بَلْ أَحْياءٌ عِنْدَ رَبِّهِمْ يُرْزَقُونَ ﴾ ـ قَالَ: أما إنَّا قَدْ سَأَلْنا عَنْ ذَلِكَ، فقال(١):

« أَرْواحُهُمْ فِي جَوْفِ طَيْرٍ خُضْرٍ، لَها قَنَادِيلُ مُعَلَّقَةٌ بِالعَرْشِ، تَسْرَحُ مِنَ الجَنَّةِ حَيْثُ شَاءَتْ، ثُمَّ تَأْوِي إِلَى تِلْكَ القَنَادِيلِ، فَاطَّلَعَ إِلَيْهِمْ رَبُّهُمْ اطَّلاعَةً فَقَالَ: هَلْ تَشْتَهُونَ شَيْئاً؟ قَالُوا: أَيَّ شَيْءٍ نَشْتَهِي، وَنَحْنُ نَسْرَحُ مِنَ الجَنَّةِ حَيْثُ شِئْنا؟ فَفَعَلَ ذَلِكَ بِهِمْ ثَلاثَ مَرَّاتٍ، فَلَمَّا رَأَوْا أَنَّهُمْ لَنْ يُتْرَكُوا مِنْ أَنْ يُسْأَلُوا، قَالُوا: يَا رَبِّ، نُرِيدُ أَنْ تَرُدَّ أَرْواحَنا

---

(١) يعني النبي صلى الله عليه وسلم. انظر النووي: (شرح صحيح مسلم). ج ٤ ص ٥٥٠.

might fight for Your sake once again. And when He saw that they were not in need of anything they were let be.

It was related by Muslim (also by at-Tirmidhī, an-Nasāʾī and Ibn Mājah).

※ ※ ※

في أَجْسادِنـا ؛حَتَّى نُقْتَلَ في سَبيلِكَ مَرَّةً أُخْرَى.
فَلَمَّا رَأَى أَنْ لَيْسَ لَهُمْ حَاجَةٌ تُرِكُوا ».

رواه مسلم (وكذلك الترمذي والنسائي وابن ماجه) .

※ ※ ※

HADITH 28

On the authority of Jundub ibn ᶜAbdullah (may Allah be pleased with him), who said that the Messenger of Allah (may the blessings and peace of Allah be upon him) said:

There was amongst those before you a man who had a wound. He was in [such] anguish that he took a knife and made with it a cut in his hand, and the blood did not cease to flow till he died. Allah the Almighty said: My servant has himself forestalled Me; I have forbidden him Paradise.

It was related by al-Bukhārī.

❊ ❊ ❊

الْحَدِيثُ الثَّامِنُ وَالْعِشْرُونَ

عَنْ جُنْدُبِ بْنِ عَبْدِ اللهِ، رَضِيَ اللهُ عَنْهُ، قَالَ: قَالَ رَسُولُ اللهِ، صَلَّى اللهُ عَلَيْهِ وَسَلَّم:

«كَانَ فِيمَنْ كَانَ قَبْلَكُمْ رَجُلٌ، بِهِ جُرْحٌ، فَجَزِعَ، فَأَخَذَ سِكِّيناً، فَحَزَّ بِهَا يَدَهُ، فَمَا رَقَأَ(١) الدَّمُ، حَتَّى مَاتَ. قَالَ اللَّهُ تَعَالَى: بَادَرَنِي عَبْدِي بِنَفْسِهِ، حَرَّمْتُ عَلَيْهِ الجَنَّةَ».

رواه البخاري.

***

---

(١) رقأ الدم: جفَّ وانقطع بعد جريانه.

HADITH 29

On the authority of Abū Hurayrah (may Allah be pleased with him) that the Messenger of Allah (may the blessings and peace of Allah be upon him) said: Allah the Almighty says:

> My faithful servant's reward from Me, if I have taken to Me his best friend from amongst the inhabitants of the world and he has then borne it patiently for My sake, shall be nothing less than Paradise.

It was related by al-Bukhārī.

※ ※ ※

الحَدِيثُ التَّاسِعُ وَالعِشْرُونَ

عَنْ أَبِي هُرَيْرَةَ، رَضِيَ اللَّهُ عَنْهُ، أَنَّ رَسُولَ اللَّهِ، صَلَّى اللَّهُ عَلَيْهِ وَسَلَّمَ، قَالَ:

« يَقُولُ اللَّهُ تَعَالَى: مَا لِعَبْدِي المُؤْمِنِ عِنْدِي جَزَاءٌ، إِذَا قَبَضْتُ صَفِيَّهُ مِنْ أَهْلِ الدُّنْيَا، ثُمَّ احْتَسَبَهُ، إِلَّا الجَنَّةُ. »

رواه البخاري.

***

HADITH 30

On the authority of Abū Hurayrah (may Allah be pleased with him), who said that the Messenger of Allah (may the blessings and peace of Allah be upon him) said: Allah (mighty and sublime be He) said:

> If My servant likes to meet Me, I like to meet him; and if he dislikes to meet Me, I dislike to meet him.

It was related by al-Bukhārī and Mālik.

A Prophetic version by Muslim which clarifies the meaning of the above Sacred Hadith reads:

On the authority of ʿĀʾishah (may Allah be pleased with her), who said that the Messenger of Allah (may the blessings and peace of Allah be upon him) said:

> He who likes to meet Allah, Allah likes to meet him; and he who dislikes to meet Allah, Allah dislikes to meet him.

I said: O Prophet of Allah, is it because of the dislike of death, for all of us dislike death? He said:

> It is not so, but rather it is that when the believer is given news of

اَلْحَدِيثُ الثَّلَاثُونَ

عَنْ أَبِي هُرَيْرَةَ ، رَضِيَ اللَّهُ عَنْهُ ، أَنَّ رَسُولَ اللَّهِ ، صَلَّى اللَّهُ عَلَيْهِ وَسَلَّمَ ، قَالَ :

« قَالَ اللَّهُ عَزَّ وَجَلَّ : إِذَا أَحَبَّ عَبْدِي لِقَائِي، أَحْبَبْتُ لِقَاءَهُ ، وَإِذَا كَرِهَ لِقَائِي، كَرِهْتُ لِقَاءَهُ » .

رواه البخاري ومالك .

وفي رواية لمسلم ، توضح معنى الحديث[1] :

عَنْ عَائِشَةَ ، رَضِيَ اللَّهُ عَنْهَا ، قَالَتْ : قَالَ رَسُولُ اللَّهِ ، صَلَّى اللَّهُ عَلَيْهِ وَسَلَّمَ :

« مَنْ أَحَبَّ لِقَاءَ اللَّهِ ، أَحَبَّ اللَّهُ لِقَاءَهُ ، وَمَنْ كَرِهَ لِقَاءَ اللَّهِ ، كَرِهَ اللَّهُ لِقَاءَهُ . فَقُلْتُ : يَا نَبِيَّ اللَّهِ ، أَكَرَاهِيَةَ الْمَوْتِ ؟ فَكُلُّنَا نَكْرَهُ الْمَوْتَ . قَالَ لَيْسَ كَذَلِكَ، وَلَكِنَّ الْمُؤْمِنَ إِذَا بُشِّرَ

---

[1] رواية مسلم ليس فيها إسناد إلى الله تعالى. والحديث بهذه الهيئة وارد في الترمذي والنسائي أيضاً .

Allah's mercy, His approval and His Paradise, he likes to meet Allah and Allah likes to meet him; but when the unbeliever is given news of Allah's punishment and His displeasure, he dislikes to meet Allah and Allah dislikes to meet him.

※ ※ ※

بِرَحْمَةِ اللَّهِ وَرِضْوَانِهِ وَجَنَّتِهِ ، أَحَبَّ لِقَاءَ اللَّهِ ، فَأَحَبَّ اللَّهُ لِقَاءَهُ ، وإِنَّ الكَافِرَ إذا بُشِّرَ بِعَذَابِ اللَّهِ وَسَخَطِهِ، كَرِهَ لِقَاءَ اللَّهِ ، وَكَرِهَ اللَّهُ لِقَاءَهُ » .

※ ※ ※

HADITH 31

On the authority of Jundub (may Allah be pleased with him), who said that the Messenger of Allah (may the blessings and peace of Allah be upon him) related:

A man said: By Allah, Allah will not forgive So-and-so. At this Allah the Almighty said: Who is he who swears by Me that I will not forgive So-and-so? Verily I have forgiven So-and-so and have nullified your [own good] deeds[1] (or as he said [it])[2].

It was related by Muslim.

* * *

---

1. A similar Hadith, which is given by Abū Dāwūd, indicates that the person referred to was a godly man whose previous good deeds were brought to nought through presuming to declare that Allah would not forgive someone's bad deeds.
2. A formula employed to cover the possibility that there might be some minor variation in the wording.

اَلْحَدِيثُ الْحَادِي وَالثَّلَاثُونَ

عَنْ جُنْدُبٍ، رَضِيَ اللَّهُ عَنْهُ:

أَنَّ رَسُولَ اللَّهِ، صَلَّى اللَّهُ عَلَيْهِ وَسَلَّمَ، حَدَّثَ «أَنَّ رَجُلاً قَالَ: وَاللَّهِ لَا يَغْفِرُ اللَّهُ لِفُلَانٍ، وَإِنَّ اللَّهَ تَعَالَى قَالَ: مَنْ ذَا الَّذِي يَتَأَلَّى(1) عَلَيَّ أَنْ لَا أَغْفِرَ لِفُلَانٍ، فَإِنِّي قَدْ غَفَرْتُ لِفُلَانٍ، وَأَحْبَطْتُ عَمَلَكَ(2)» أَوْ كَمَا قَالَ.

رواه مسلم.

***

---

(1) يتألَّى: يحلف.
(2) وفي رواية لأبي داود، ما يدل على أنّ الرجل الذي تألى على الله ألا يغفر لفلان، كان مجتهداً في العبادة، ولكن الله أحبط عمله لتأليه على الله بعدم المغفرة.

HADITH 32

On the authority of Abū Hurayrah (may Allah be pleased with him) from the Prophet (may the blessings and peace of Allah be upon him), who said:

A man sinned greatly against himself, and when death came to him he charged his sons, saying: When I have died, burn me, then crush me and scatter [my ashes] into the sea, for, by Allah, if my Lord takes possession of me, He will punish me in a manner in which He has punished no one [else]. So they did that to him. Then He said to the earth: Produce what you have taken — and there he was! And He said to him: What induced you to do what you did? He said: Being afraid of You, O my Lord (or he said: Being frightened of You[1]) and because of that He forgave him.

It was related by Muslim (also by al-Bukhārī, an-Nasāʾī and Ibn Mājah).

---

1. An alternative wording.

الحديث الثاني والثلاثون

عَنْ أبي هُرَيْرَةَ رَضِيَ اللَّهُ عَنْهُ، عَنِ النَّبِيِّ، صَلَّى اللَّهُ عَلَيْهِ وَسَلَّمَ، قَالَ:

«أَسْرَفَ رَجُلٌ عَلَى نَفْسِهِ، فَلَمَّا حَضَرَهُ المَوْتُ أَوْصَى بَنِيهِ، فَقَالَ: إذا أَنَا مُتُّ فَأَحْرِقُونِي، ثُمَّ اسْحَقُونِي، ثُمَّ أَذْرُونِي في البَحْرِ فَوَاللَّهِ لَئِنْ قَدَرَ عَلَيَّ رَبِّي لَيُعَذِّبَنِي عَذاباً، ما عَذَّبَهُ أَحَداً، فَفَعَلُوا ذَلِكَ بِهِ. فَقَالَ لِلأَرْضِ(١): أَدِّي ما أَخَذْتِ، فَإذا هُوَ قَائِمٌ، فَقَالَ لَهُ: ما حَمَلَكَ عَلَى ما صَنَعْتَ؟ قَالَ: خَشْيَتُكَ يَا رَبِّ، أوْ مَخَافَتُكَ. فَغَفَرَ لَهُ بِذَلِكَ».

رواه مسلم (وكذلك البخاري والنسائي وابن ماجه).

---

(١) أي قال الله تعالى.

HADITH 33

On the authority of Abū Hurayrah (may Allah be pleased with him) that the Prophet (may the blessings and peace of Allah be upon him), from among the things he reports from his Lord (mighty and sublime be He), is that he said:

A servant [of Allah's] committed a sin and said: O Allah, forgive me my sin. And He (glorified and exalted be He) said: My servant has committed a sin and has known that he has a Lord who forgives sins and punishes for them. Then he sinned again and said: O Lord, forgive me my sin. And He (glorified and exalted be He) said: My servant has committed a sin and has known that he has a Lord who forgives sins and punishes for them. Then he sinned again and said: O Lord, forgive me my sin. And He (glorified and exalted be He) said: My servant has committed a sin and has known that he has a Lord who forgives sins and punishes for sins. Do what you wish, for I have forgiven you.

It was related by Muslim (also by al-Bukhārī).

※ ※ ※

الحَدِيثُ الثَّالِثُ وَالثَّلَاثُونَ

عَنْ أَبِي هُرَيْرَةَ، رَضِيَ اللهُ عَنْهُ، عَنِ النَّبِيِّ صَلَّى اللهُ عَلَيْهِ وَسَلَّمَ، فِيمَا يَحْكِي عَنْ رَبِّهِ عَزَّ وَجَلَّ، قَالَ:

« أَذْنَبَ عَبْدٌ ذَنْباً، فَقَالَ: اللَّهُمَّ. اغْفِرْ لِي ذَنْبِي، فَقَالَ تَبَارَكَ وَتَعَالَى: أَذْنَبَ عَبْدِي ذَنْباً، فَعَلِمَ أَنَّ لَهُ رَبّاً، يَغْفِرُ الذَّنْبَ، وَيَأْخُذُ بِهِ. ثُمَّ عَادَ فَأَذْنَبَ، فَقَالَ: أَيْ رَبِّ، اغْفِرْ لِي ذَنْبِي، فَقَالَ تَبَارَكَ وَتَعَالَى: عَبْدِي أَذْنَبَ ذَنْباً. فَعَلِمَ أَنَّ لَهُ رَبّاً يَغْفِرُ الذَّنْبَ، وَيَأْخُذُ بِهِ. ثُمَّ عَادَ فَأَذْنَبَ، فَقَالَ: أَيْ رَبِّ، اغْفِرْ لِي ذَنْبِي، فَقَالَ تَبَارَكَ وَتَعَالَى: أَذْنَبَ عَبْدِي ذَنْباً، فَعَلِمَ أَنَّ لَهُ رَبّاً، يَغْفِرُ الذَّنْبَ، وَيَأْخُذُ بِالذَّنْبِ. اعْمَلْ مَا شِئْتَ، فَقَدْ غَفَرْتُ لَكَ ».

رواه مسلم (وكذلك البخاري).

***

HADITH 34

On the authority of Anas (may Allah be pleased with him), who said: I heard the Messenger of Allah (may the blessings and peace of Allah be upon him) say: Allah the Almighty said:

> O son of Adam, so long as you call upon Me and ask of Me, I shall forgive you for what you have done, and I shall not mind. O son of Adam, were your sins to reach the clouds of the sky and were you then to ask forgiveness of Me, I would forgive you. O son of Adam, were you to come to Me with sins nearly as great as the earth and were you then to face Me, ascribing no partner to Me, I would bring you forgiveness nearly as great as it[1].

It was related by at-Tirmidhī (also by Aḥmad ibn Ḥanbal). Its chain of authorities is sound.

---

1. i.e. as the earth, meaning that Allah will forgive in like measure to man's sins.

الحديث الرابع والثلاثون

عَنْ أَنَسٍ، رَضِيَ اللَّهُ عَنْهُ، قَالَ: سَمِعْتُ رَسُولَ اللَّهِ، صَلَّى اللَّهُ عَلَيْهِ وَسَلَّمَ، يَقُولُ:

« قَالَ اللَّهُ تَعَالَى: يَا ابْنَ آدَمَ، إِنَّكَ مَا دَعَوْتَنِي وَرَجَوْتَنِي، غَفَرْتُ لَكَ عَلَى مَا كَانَ مِنْكَ وَلَا أُبَالِي. يَا ابْنَ آدَمَ: لَوْ بَلَغَتْ ذُنُوبُكَ عَنَانَ السَّمَاءِ ثُمَّ اسْتَغْفَرْتَنِي، غَفَرْتُ لَكَ. يَا ابْنَ آدَمَ: إِنَّكَ لَوْ أَتَيْتَنِي بِقُرَابِ الْأَرْضِ خَطَايَا ثُمَّ لَقِيتَنِي لَا تُشْرِكُ بِي شَيْئاً، لَأَتَيْتُكَ بِقُرَابِهَا مَغْفِرَةً ».

رواه الترمذي (وكذلك أحمد) وسنده حسن(1).

---

(١) انظر الألباني :(الأحاديث الصحيحة) حديث رقم ١٢٧. جـ ١ ص ٣٩ - النووي : (رياض الصالحين) باب الاستغفار. حديث ١٨٧٦.

HADITH 35

On the authority of Abū Hurayrah (may Allah be pleased with him), who said that the Messenger of Allah (may the blessings and peace of Allah be upon him) said:

Our Lord (glorified and exalted be He) descends each night to the earth's sky when there remains the final third of the night, and He says: Who is saying a prayer to Me that I may answer it? Who is asking something of Me that I may give it him? Who is asking forgiveness of Me that I may forgive him?

It was related by al-Bukhārī (also by Muslim, Mālik, at-Tirmidhī and Abū Dāwūd).

In a version by Muslim the Hadith ends with the words:

And thus He continues till [the light of] dawn shines.

※ ※ ※

الحَديثُ الخَامِسُ وَالثَّلاثونَ

عَنْ أبي هُرَيْرَةَ، رَضِيَ اللهُ عَنْهُ، أَنَّ رَسُولَ اللهِ، صَلَّى اللهُ عَلَيْهِ وَسَلَّمَ، قَالَ:

« يَتَنَزَّلُ رَبُّنا، تَبَارَكَ وَتعالى، كُلَّ لَيْلَةٍ إلى سَماءِ الدُّنْيا، حينَ يَبْقَى ثُلُثُ اللَّيلِ الآخِرُ، فَيَقُولُ: مَنْ يَدْعُوني فأَسْتَجِيبَ لَهُ؟ مَنْ يَسْأَلُني فَأُعْطِيَهُ؟ مَنْ يَسْتَغْفِرُني فأَغْفِرَ لَهُ؟ »

رواه البخاري (وكذلك مسلم ومالك والترمذي وأبو داود).

وفي رواية لمسلم زيادة:

« فَلا يَزالُ كذَلِك حَتَّى يُضِيءَ الفَجرُ ».

※ ※ ※

HADITH 36

On the authority of Anas (may Allah be pleased with him) from the Prophet (may the blessings and peace of Allah be upon him), who said:

The believers will gather together on the Day of Resurrection and will say: Should we not ask [someone] to intercede for us with our Lord? So they will come to Adam and will say: You are the Father of mankind; Allah created you with His hand and He made His angels bow down to you and He taught you the names of everything, so intercede for us with your Lord so that He may give us relief from this place where we are. And he will say: I am not in a position [to do that] — and he will mention his wrongdoing and will feel ashamed and will say: Go to Noah, for he is the first messenger that Allah sent to the inhabitants of the earth. So they will come to him and he will say: I am not in a position [to do that] — and he will mention his having requested something of his Lord about

الحديث السادس والثلاثون

عَنْ أَنَسٍ، رَضِيَ اللهُ عَنْهُ، عَنِ النَّبِيِّ صَلَّى اللهُ عَلَيْهِ وَسَلَّمَ، قَالَ:

« يَجْتَمِعُ المُؤْمِنُونَ يَوْمَ القِيَامَةِ فَيَقُولُونَ: لَوِ اسْتَشْفَعْنَا إِلَى رَبِّنَا، فَيَأْتُونَ آدَمَ، فَيَقُولُونَ: أَنْتَ أَبُو النَّاسِ، خَلَقَكَ اللهُ بِيَدِهِ، وَأَسْجَدَ لَكَ مَلَائِكَتَهُ، وَعَلَّمَكَ أَسْمَاءَ كُلِّ شَيْءٍ، فَاشْفَعْ لَنَا عِنْدَ رَبِّكَ، حَتَّى يُرِيحَنَا مِنْ مَكَانِنَا هَذَا، فَيَقُولُ: لَسْتُ هُنَاكُمْ ـ وَيَذْكُرُ ذَنْبَهُ، فَيَسْتَحْيِي ـ ائْتُوا نُوحاً؛ فَإِنَّهُ أَوَّلُ رَسُولٍ بَعَثَهُ اللهُ إِلَى أَهْلِ الأَرْضِ، فَيَأْتُونَهُ، فَيَقُولُ: لَسْتُ هُنَاكُمْ ـ ويَذْكُرُ سُؤَالَهُ رَبَّهُ مَا لَيْسَ لَهُ بِهِ عِلْمٌ [1]،

---

[1] إشارة إلى مفهوم قوله تعالى: ﴿ وَنَادَىٰ نُوحٌ رَّبَّهُ فَقَالَ رَبِّ إِنَّ ٱبْنِي مِنْ أَهْلِي وَإِنَّ وَعْدَكَ ٱلْحَقُّ وَأَنتَ أَحْكَمُ ٱلْحَاكِمِينَ ۞ قَالَ يَا نُوحُ إِنَّهُ لَيْسَ مِنْ أَهْلِكَ إِنَّهُ عَمَلٌ غَيْرُ صَالِحٍ فَلَا تَسْأَلْنِ مَا لَيْسَ لَكَ بِهِ عِلْمٌ إِنِّي أَعِظُكَ أَن تَكُونَ مِنَ ٱلْجَاهِلِينَ ﴾ هود ١١: ٤٥ ـ ٤٦.

which he had no [proper] knowledge[1], and he will feel ashamed and will say: Go to the Friend of the Merciful[2]. So they will come to him and he will say: I am not in a positon [to do that]. Go to Moses, a servant to whom Allah talked and to whom He gave the Torah. So they will come to him and he will say: I am not in a position [to do that] — and he will mention the taking of a life other than for a life[3], and he will feel ashamed in the sight of his Lord and will say: Go to Jesus, Allah's servant and messenger, Allah's word and spirit. So they will come to him and he will say: I am not in a position [to do that]. Go to Muḥammad (may the blessings and peace of Allah be upon him), a servant to whom Allah has forgiven all his

---

1. This is a reference to the Qurʾān, Chapter 11, Verses 45 and 46, in which Noah asks the Almighty to save his son from the Flood and is told that his son is not a righteous person and that he, Noah, should not expect him to be saved merely because he is his son.

2. i.e. Abraham.

3. This is a reference to the Qurʾān, Chapter 28, Verses 15 and 16, where it is told how Moses, coming to the help of one of his followers who is fighting with another man, strikes the other man, who dies from the blow.

فَيَسْتَحْيِي ـ فَيَقُولُ : ائْتُوا خَلِيلَ الرَّحْمَنِ (١) . فَيَأْتُونَهُ ، فَيَقُولُ : لَسْتُ هُنَاكُمْ ، ائْتُوا مُوسَى ، عَبْداً كَلَّمَهُ اللهُ ، وَأَعْطَاهُ التَّوْرَاةَ . فَيَأْتُونَهُ ، فَيَقُولُ : لَسْتُ هُنَاكُمْ ـ وَيَذْكُرُ قَتْلَ النَّفْسِ بِغَيْرِ نَفْسٍ (٢)، فَيَسْتَحْيِي مِنْ رَبِّهِ ـ فَيَقُولُ : ائْتُوا عِيسَى، عَبْدَ اللهِ وَرَسُولَهُ ، وَكَلِمَةَ اللهِ وَرُوحَهُ . فَيَأْتُونَهُ ، فَيَقُولُ : لَسْتُ هُنَاكُمْ ، ائْتُوا مُحَمَّداً ، ـ صَلَّى اللهُ عَلَيْهِ وَسَلَّمَ ـ عَبْداً غَفَرَ اللهُ لَهُ مَا تَقَدَّمَ

---

(١) أي إبراهيم عليه السلام .
(٢) إشارة إلى قتل موسى عليه السلام رجلاً من عدوه كان يقتتل مع رجل من شيعته (سورة القصص ٢٨ : ١٥ ـ ١٦) .

133

wrongdoing, past and future. So they will come to me and I shall set forth to ask permission to come to my Lord, and permission will be given, and when I shall see my Lord I shall prostrate myself. He will leave me thus for such time as it pleases Him, then it will be said [to me]: Raise your head. Ask and it will be granted. Speak and it will be heard. Intercede and your intercession will be accepted. So I shall raise my head and praise Him with a form of praise that He will teach me. Then I shall intercede and He will set me a limit [as to the number of people], so I shall admit them into Paradise. Then I shall return to Him, and when I shall see my Lord [I shall bow down] as before. Then I shall intercede and He will set me a limit [as to the number of people]. So I shall admit them into Paradise. Then I shall return for a third time, then a fourth, and I shall say: There remains in Hell-fire only those whom the Qur'ān has confined[1] and who must be there for eternity.

---

1. i.e. those referred to in the Qur'ān as "abiding therein for ever".

مِنْ ذَنْبِهِ وَمَا تَأَخَّرَ ، فَيَأْتُونَنِي ، فَأَنْطَلِقُ حَتَّى أَسْتَأْذِنَ عَلَى رَبِّي فَيُؤْذَنُ . فَإِذَا رَأَيْتُ رَبِّي وَقَعْتُ سَاجِداً ، فَيَدَعُنِي مَا شَاءَ اللَّهُ ، ثُمَّ يُقَالُ : ارْفَعْ رَأْسَكَ، وَسَلْ تُعْطَهْ ، وَقُلْ يُسْمَعْ ، وَاشْفَعْ تُشَفَّعْ . فَأَرْفَعُ رَأْسِي ، فَأَحْمَدُهُ بِتَحْمِيدٍ يُعَلِّمُنِيهِ ، ثُمَّ أَشْفَعُ ، فَيَحُدُّ لِي حَدّاً ، فَأُدْخِلُهُمُ الْجَنَّةَ. ثُمَّ أَعُودُ إِلَيْهِ ، فَإِذَا رَأَيْتُ رَبِّي [فَأَقَعُ سَاجِداً](1) مِثْلَهُ ، ثُمَّ أَشْفَعُ فَيَحُدُّ لِي حَدّاً ، فَأُدْخِلُهُمُ الْجَنَّةَ.ثُمَّ أَعُودُ الثَّالِثَةَ،ثُمَّ أَعُودُ الرَّابِعَةَ ، فَأَقُولُ : مَا بَقِيَ فِي النَّارِ إِلَّا مَنْ حَبَسَهُ الْقُرْآنُ(2) ، وَوَجَبَ عَلَيْهِ الْخُلُودُ » .

---

(1) ما بين القوسين مضاف من رواية أخرى للبخاري (كتاب الرقاق : باب صفة الجنة والنار) لتوضيح السياق . والمعنى أن الرسول صلى الله عليه وسلم يقع ساجداً مثلما صنع من قبل.
(2) قال أبو عبد الله البخاري : (إلا من حبسه القرآن) يعني قول الله تعالى : ﴿خَالِدِينَ فِيهَا﴾ .

It was related by al-Bukhārī (also by Muslim, at-Tirmidhī, and Ibn Mājah).

Another version by al-Bukhārī adds:
The Prophet (may the blessings and peace of Allah be upon him) said:

There shall come out of Hell-fire he who has said: *There is no god but Allah* and who has in his heart goodness weighing a barley-corn; then there shall come out of Hell-fire he who has said: *There is no god but Allah* and who has in his heart goodness weighing a grain of wheat; then there shall come out of Hell-fire he who has said: *There is no god but Allah* and who has in his heart goodness weighing an atom.

※ ※ ※

رواه البخاري (وكذلك مسلم والترمذي وابن ماجه) .
وفي رواية أخرى للبخاري زيادة هي :

قَالَ النَّبِيُّ صَلَّى اللَّهُ عَلَيْهِ وَسَلَّمَ: يَخْرُجُ مِنَ النَّارِ مَنْ قَالَ : لَا إِلٰهَ إِلَّا اللَّهُ ، وَكَانَ فِي قَلْبِهِ مِنَ الخَيْرِ مَا يَزِنُ شَعِيرَةً ، ثُمَّ يَخْرُجُ مِنَ النَّارِ مَنْ قَالَ : لَا إِلٰهَ إِلَّا اللَّهُ ، وَكَانَ فِي قَلْبِهِ مِنَ الخَيْرِ مَا يَزِنُ بُرَّةً ، ثُمَّ يَخْرُجُ مِنَ النَّارِ مَنْ قَالَ : لَا إِلٰهَ إِلَّا اللَّهُ ، وَكَانَ فِي قَلْبِهِ مَا يَزِنُ مِنَ الخَيْرِ ذَرَّةً » .

✸ ✸ ✸

HADITH 37

On the authority of Abū Hurayrah (may Allah be pleased with him), who said that the Messenger of Allah (may the blessings and peace of Allah be upon him) said: Allah said:

I have prepared for My righteous servants what no eye has seen and no ear has heard, nor has it occurred to human heart. Thus recite if you wish[1]: **And no soul knows what joy for them[2] has been kept hidden.**[3]

It was related by al-Bukhārī, Muslim, at-Tirmidhī and Ibn Mājah.

* * *

---

1. The words "Thus recite if you wish" are those of Abū Hurayrah.
2. i.e. the inhabitants of Paradise.
3. Qurʾān: Chapter 32, Verse 17.

الْحَدِيثُ السَّابِعُ وَالثَّلَاثُونَ

عَنْ أَبِي هُرَيْرَةَ، رَضِيَ اللَّهُ عَنْهُ، قَالَ: قَالَ رَسُولُ اللَّهِ، صَلَّى اللَّهُ عَلَيْهِ وَسَلَّمَ:

«قَالَ اللَّهُ: أَعْدَدْتُ لِعِبَادِي الصَّالِحِينَ مَا لَا عَيْنٌ رَأَتْ، وَلَا أُذُنٌ سَمِعَتْ، وَلَا خَطَرَ عَلَى قَلْبِ بَشَرٍ». فَاقْرَأُوا إِنْ شِئْتُمْ[1]: ﴿فَلَا تَعْلَمُ نَفْسٌ مَا أُخْفِيَ لَهُمْ مِنْ قُرَّةِ أَعْيُنٍ﴾[2].

رواه البخاري ومسلم والترمذي وابن ماجه.

***

---

[1] هذه الجملة (فاقرأوا إن شئتم) من كلام أبي هريرة كما ورد في رواية أخرى للبخاري.
[2] السجدة ٣٢: ١٧.

HADITH 38

On the authority of Abū Hurayrah (may Allah be pleased with him), from the Messenger of Allah (may the blessings and peace of Allah be upon him), who said:

When Allah created Paradise and Hell-fire, He sent Gabriel to Paradise, saying: Look at it and at what I have prepared therein for its inhabitants. He said:[1] So he came to it and looked at it and at what Allah had prepared therein for its inhabitants. He said[1]: So he returned to Him and said: By Your glory, no one hears of it without entering it. So He ordered that it be encompassed by forms of hardship[2], and He said: Return to it and look at what I have prepared therein for its inhabitants. He said:[1] So he returned to it and found that it was encompassed by forms of hardship. Then he returned to Him and said: By Your glory, I fear that no one will enter it. He said: Go to

---
1. i.e. the Prophet.
2. The Arabic word used here is *makārih*, the literal meaning of which is "things that are disliked". In this context it refers to forms of religious discipline, positive and negative, that man usually finds onerous.

اَلْحَدِيثُ الثَّامِنُ وَالثَّلَاثُونَ

عَنْ أَبِي هُرَيْرَةَ، رَضِيَ اللَّهُ عَنْهُ، عَنْ رَسُولِ اللَّهِ، صَلَّى اللَّهُ عَلَيْهِ وَسَلَّمَ، قَالَ:

«لَمَّا خَلَقَ اللَّهُ الجَنَّةَ وَالنَّارَ، أَرْسَلَ جِبْرِيلَ إِلَى الجَنَّةِ، فَقَالَ: انْظُرْ إِلَيْهَا، وَإِلَى ما أَعْدَدْتُ لِأَهْلِها فِيها. قَالَ: فَجَاءَهَا وَنَظَرَ إِلَيْهَا وَإِلَى مَا أَعَدَّ اللَّهُ لِأَهْلِهَا فِيها. قَالَ: فَرَجَعَ إِلَيْهِ، قَالَ: فَوَعِزَّتِكَ لَا يَسْمَعُ بِهَا أَحَدٌ إِلَّا دَخَلَها. فَأَمَرَ بِهَا فَحُفَّتْ بِالمَكَارِهِ، فَقَالَ: ارْجِعْ إِلَيْهَا، فَانْظُرْ إِلَى مَا أَعْدَدْتُ لِأَهْلِها فِيها، قَالَ: فَرَجَعَ إِلَيْهَا، فَإِذَا هِيَ قَدْ حُفَّتْ بِالمَكَارِهِ، فَرَجَعَ إِلَيْهِ، فَقَالَ: وَعِزَّتِكَ لَقَدْ خِفْتُ أَنْ لَا يَدْخُلَهَا أَحَدٌ قَالَ: اذْهَبْ إِلَى النَّارِ

Hell-fire and look at it and at what I have prepared therein for its inhabitants, and he found that it was in layers, one above the other. Then he returned to Him and said: By Your glory, no one who hears of it will enter it. So He ordered that it be encompassed by lusts. Then He said: Return to it. And he returned to it and said: By Your glory, I am frightened that no one will escape from entering it.

It was related by at-Tirmidhī, who said that it was a good and sound Hadith (also by Abū Dāwūd and an-Nasāʾī).

※ ※ ※

فَانْظُرْ إِلَيْهَا ، وَإِلَى مَا أَعْدَدْتُ لِأَهْلِهَا فِيهَا . فَإِذَا هِيَ يَرْكَبُ بَعْضُهَا بَعْضَاً ، فَرَجَعَ إِلَيْهِ ، فَقَالَ : وَعِزَّتِكَ لاَ يَسْمَعُ بِهَا أَحَدٌ فَيَدْخُلَهَا . فَأَمَرَ بِهَا فَحُفَّتْ بِالشَّهَوَاتِ ، فَقَالَ : ارْجِعْ إِلَيْهَا ، فَرَجَعَ إِلَيْهَا ، فَقَالَ : وَعِزَّتِكَ لَقَدْ خَشِيتُ أَنْ لاَ يَنْجُوَ مِنْهَا أَحَدٌ إِلاَّ دَخَلَهَا » .

رواه الترمذي وقال حديث حسن صحيح . (وكذلك أبو داود والنسائي) .

***

HADITH 39

On the authority of Abū Saʿīd al-Khudrī (may Allah be pleased with him) from the Prophet (may the blessings and peace of Allah be upon him), who said:

Paradise and Hell-fire disputed together, and Hell-fire said: In me are the mighty and the haughty. Paradise said: In me are the weak and the poor. So Allah judged between them, [saying]: You are Paradise, My mercy; through you I show mercy to those I wish. And you are Hell-fire, My punishment; through you I punish those I wish, and it is incumbent upon Me that each of you shall have its fill.

It was related by Muslim (also by al-Bukhārī and at-Tirmidhī).

※ ※ ※

الحَدِيثُ التَّاسِعُ وَالثَّلَاثُونَ

عَنْ أبي سَعيدٍ الخُدْريّ، رَضِيَ اللهُ عَنْهُ، عنِ النَّبيِّ صَلَّى اللهُ عَلَيْهِ وَسَلَّمَ، قَالَ:

« احْتَجَّتِ الجَنَّةُ والنَّارُ. فقَالتِ النَّارُ: فِيَّ الجَبَّارونَ والمُتكَبِّرونَ. وَقالتِ الجَنَّةُ: فِيَّ ضُعَفاءُ النَّاسِ ومَساكينُهُمْ. فقَضَى اللهُ بَيْنَهُما: إنَّكِ الجَنَّةُ رَحْمَتي، أَرْحَمُ بِكِ مَنْ أشاءُ، وإنَّكِ النَّارُ عَذابي، أُعذِّبُ بِكِ مَنْ أشاءُ، ولِكلَيْكُما عَلَيَّ مِلْؤُها. »

رواه مسلم (وكذلك البخاري والترمذي).

***

HADITH 40

On the authority of Abū Saʿīd al-Khudrī (may Allah be pleased with him), who said that the Prophet (may the blessings and peace of Allah be upon him) said:

Allah will say to the inhabitants of Paradise: O inhabitants of Paradise! They will say: O our Lord, we present ourselves and are at Your pleasure, and goodness rests in Your hands. Then He will say: Are you contented? And they will say: And how should we not be contented, O Lord, when You have given to us that which You have given to no one else of Your creation? Then He will say: Would you not like Me to give you something better than that? And they will say: O Lord and what thing is better than that? And He will say: I shall cause My favour to descend upon you and thereafter shall never be displeased with you.

It was related by al-Bukhārī (also by Muslim and at-Tirmidhī).

※ ※ ※

الحديث الأربعون

عَنْ أبي سَعيدٍ الخُدْريّ، رَضِيَ اللَّهُ عَنْهُ، قالَ: قالَ النَّبِيُّ، صَلَّى اللَّهُ عَلَيْهِ وَسَلَّمَ:

«إنَّ اللَّهَ يَقولُ لأهْلِ الجَنَّةِ: يا أهْلَ الجَنَّةِ. فَيَقُولون: لَبَّيْكَ رَبَّنا وسَعْدَيْكَ، والخَيْرُ في يَدَيْكَ، فَيَقُولُ: هَلْ رَضِيتُمْ؟ فَيَقُولون: وَما لَنا لاَ نَرْضى يا رَبِّ، وَقَدْ أعْطَيْتَنا ما لَمْ تُعْطِ أحَداً مِنْ خَلْقِكَ. فَيَقُولُ: ألا أعْطِيكُمْ أفْضَلَ مِنْ ذَلِكَ؟ فَيَقُولونَ: يا رَبِّ وأيُّ شَيءٍ أفْضَلُ مِنْ ذَلِكَ؟ فَيَقُولُ: أُحِلُّ عَلَيْكُمْ رِضْواني، فَلا أسْخَطُ عَلَيكُمْ بَعْدَهُ أبداً».

رواه البخاري (وكذلك مسلم والترمذي).

***

INDEX - فهرس

رقم الحديث Hadith No.	أطراف الأحاديث أو عباراتها المتميزة Opening words or distinguishing phrase	صفحة Page
1	لمّا قضى الله الخلق.. When Allah decreed the Creation..	40/41
2	كذبني ابن آدم .. The son of Adam denied Me..	42/43
3	أصبح من عبادي مؤمن بي وكافر .. This morning one of My servants became..	44/45
4	يسب بنو آدم الدهر.. Sons of Adam inveigh against..	48/49
5	أنا أغنى الشركاء .. I am so self-sufficient..	50/51
6	إن أول الناس يقضى .. عليه .. The first of people against whom..	52/53
7	يعجب ربك من راعي غنم .. Your Lord delights at a shepherd..	56/57
8	من صلّى صلاة لم يقرأ فيها بأمّ القرآن .. A prayer performed by someone..	58/59
9	إن أول ما يحاسب به العبد .. The first of his actions..	62/63

Hadith No.		Page
10	الصوم لي .. Fasting is Mine..	64/65
11	أنفق يا ابن آدم .. Spend, O son of Adam..	66/67
12	حوسب رجل ممّن كان قبلكم .. A man from.. those who were before you..	68/69
13	فجاءه رجلان : أحدهما يشكو العيْلة .. .. and there came to him two men..	70/71
14	إن الله تبارك وتعالى ملائكة .. Allah.. has angels..	74/75
15	أنا عند ظن عبدي بي .. I am as My servant thinks I am..	78/79
16	إن الله كتب الحسنات .. Allah has written down the good deeds..	80/81
17	يا عبادي : إني حرمت الظلم .. O My servants, I have forbidden oppression..	82/83
18	يا ابن آدم : مرضت فلم تعدني .. O son of Adam, I fell ill..	88/89
19	الكبرياء ردائي .. Pride is My cloak..	92/93
20	تفتح أبواب الجنة .. The gates of Paradise will be opened..	94/95
21	ثلاثة أنا خصمهم .. There are three whose adversary I shall be..	96/97

149

Hadith No.		Page
22	لا يحقر أحدكم نفسه .. Let not anyone of you belittle himself..	98/99
23	أين المتحابون بجلالي .. Where are those who love one another..	100/101
24	إن الله إذا أحب عبداً .. If Allah has loved a servant..	102/103
25	من عادى لي ولياً .. Whosoever shows enmity..	104/105
26	إن أغبط أوليائي عندي .. Truly of those devoted to Me..	106/107
27	أرواحهم في جوف طير خضر .. Their souls are in the insides of green birds..	108/109
28	كان فيمن كان قبلكم رجل به جرح .. There was .. a man who had a wound..	112/113
29	ما لعبدي المؤمن عندي جزاء .. My faithful servant's reward..	114/115
30	إذا أحب عبدي لقائي .. If My servant likes to meet Me..	116/117
31	من ذا الذي يتألّى عليّ .. Who is he who swears by Me..	120/121
32	أسرف رجل على نفسه .. A man sinned greatly against himself..	122/123
33	أذنب عبد ذنباً .. A servant of Allah's committed a sin..	124/125

150

Hadith No.		Page
34	يا ابن آدم إنك ما دعوتني .. O son of Adam, so long as you call upon Me..	126/127
35	يتنزل ربنا تبارك وتعالى كل ليلة .. Our Lord.. descends each night..	128/129
36	لو أستشفعنا إلى ربنا .. Should we not ask someone to intercede for us..	130/131
37	أعددت لعبادي الصالحين .. I have prepared for My righteous servants..	138/139
38	لـمَّا خلق الله الجنة والنار .. When Allah created Paradise and Hell-fire..	140/141
39	احتجت الجنة والنار .. Paradise and Hell-fire disputed together..	144/145
40	إن الله يقول لأهل الجنة .. Allah will say to the inhabitants of Paradise..	146/147

✵✵✵